Cakaulevu Reef
DRUA
DRUA
TUTU
Navukebuli
VANUA LEVU
Sese
Labasa
Saqani
RABI
Dikeva
▲ 957 m
utari
Natewa Bay
KIOA
oloa
Buca
Natuvu
Naselesele
LAUCALA
avu
Bagasau
Somosomo
QAMEA
Somosomo
Wairiki
Bouma
Somosomo
TAVEUNI
Navakawau

VANUA
BALAVU
Mavana
YACATA
KANACEA
Lomaloma
Nasau
KORO
MAGO
IVITI
LAU
OUP
Koro Sea
GROUP
CICIA
uloa
Mabula
NAIRAI
NAYAU
iti
Liku
AU
Lakeba Passage
LAKEBA
Tubou

LAU
GROUP
Naroi
MOALA

Naikeleyaga
TOTOYA
KABARA
Bounty Boat Passage
OGEA
LEVU
FULAGA
MATUKU

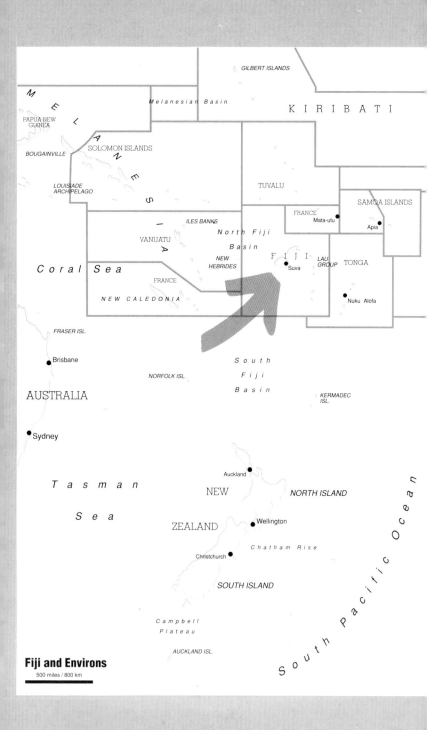

Fiji and Environs

500 miles / 800 km

FIJI ISLANDS

Written and Presented by **James Siers**

INSIGHT
POCKET
GUIDES

Insight Pocket Guide:

Fiji Islands

Directed by
Hans Höfer

Managing Editor
Francis Dorai

Photography by
James Siers

Design Concept by
V. Barl

Design by
Laddawan Wong

© 1994 APA Publications (HK) Ltd

All Rights Reserved

Printed in Singapore by
Höfer Press (Pte) Ltd
Fax: 65-8616438

Distributed in the United States by
Houghton Mifflin Company
222 Berkeley Street
Boston, Massachusetts 02116-3764
ISBN: 0-395-69021-8

Distributed in Canada by
Thomas Allen & Son
390 Steelcase Road East
Markham, Ontario L3R 1G2
ISBN: 0-395-69021-8

Distributed in the UK & Ireland by
GeoCenter International UK Ltd
The Viables Center, Harrow Way
Basingstoke, Hampshire RG22 4BJ
ISBN: 9-62421-591-X

Worldwide distribution enquiries:
Höfer Communications Pte Ltd
38 Joo Koon Road
Singapore 2262
ISBN: 9-62421-591-X

 Welcome! I first came to Fiji in 1962 on a photo-journalism assignment. I was immediately captivated by the striking scenery, the gracious people and Fiji's romantic past. A decision had just been made by the British colonial administration to open Fiji to tourism, but the problems were manifold. Fiji was off the beaten track and on the 'other' side of the world. There was virtually no tourist infrastructure. Only one resort hotel existed on the Coral Coast. In the 30 years since that first visit, I became a frequent visitor, to write and photograph several books on the islands as well as to direct films. After returning almost every year, in 1984 I decided this was the place I would settle in.

Mine was never a superficial interest. I wanted to know everything about Fiji in the broader context of its place in the South Pacific. To prove a historical point, in 1976 I sailed in a native Micronesian canoe, 1,000 nautical miles from the Gilbert Islands to Fiji, showing without doubt that such voyages in the past could easily have been accomplished. For the less adventurous traveller, I've designed special day itineraries that explore the main island of Viti Levu. A series of *Pick & Mix* options, in and outside Viti Levu, offer more diversions while those with more time on their hands will appreciate the *Excursions* section, with visits to outer islands, to exclusive resorts, cruises, village stays, hiking, diving and deep sea fishing trips. Select as few or as many of the itineraries as you wish. Together, they represent the best of what Fiji's 300 islands have to offer.

Much has changed since 1962 but happily not the Fijian people whose friendliness and hospitality is legendary. Though tourism has been developed, it is still minuscule compared to other places. There are no gigantic hotels; many resorts are family owned and managed, and offer the kind of intimacy impossible to experience elsewhere. This is what makes Fiji special. Here you are not a cipher to be processed and sent home again but a special guest to be looked after and honoured.

Welcome! Bula! — James Siers

CONTENTS

Welcome **5**

History and Culture
Point of Origin **12**
European Contact...............................**14**
Cannibals..**15**
New Trade **16**
Tongan Influence................................**17**
Cession to British **17**
Military Coups **17**
Fijian Culture **18**
Historical Highlights **19**

Day Itineraries
Day 1: Day Cruise to Mamanutha Islands..**21**
Day 2: Sleeping Giant
and Viseisei Village......................**23**
Day 3: Nadi to Suva................................**26**

Pick & Mix
1. Suva..**30**
2. Natadola Beach Picnic
and Coral Coast Railway......................**32**
3. Nausori Highlands **34**
4. Levuka: Fiji's Old Capital....................**38**
5. Ba River Run **40**
6. Navua River Trip................................**41**

Excursions
7. Namuamua Village Stay **44**
8. Mamanutha Islands:
Beachcomber Resort **46**
9. Yasawas: The Blue Lagoon Cruise **48**
10. Viti Levu: Interior Hike **51**
11. Exploring Fiji's North **55**
12. Toberua Island Resort.........................**60**

Activities
13. Scuba Diving **62**
14. Fishing..**64**

Shopping **66**

Eating Out **70**

Nightlife **75**

Calendar of Special Events..............**78**

*Preceding pages: Yachts at
anchor, Mamanutha Islands*   **8**

Practical Information

Getting There **80**
Arriving...**80**
Travel Essentials **80**
When to Visit **80**
Climate and Clothing **81**
Visa and Passports, Vaccinations,
Customs, Electricity, Time Differences **82**
Getting Acquainted............................**82**
Geography **82**
Population and People, Religion,
Language...**83**
Money Matters **84**
Currency, Credit Cards and Banks,
Business Hours, Tipping.......................**84**
Getting Around **85**
Bus, Taxi, Car, Ferry, Domestic Air.........**85**
Accommodation...................................**86**
Health & Emergencies **89**
Police, Robbery **89**
Accident and Illness,
Emergency numbers **90**
Media & Communication......................**90**
Postal Services, Telecommunications **90**
Media..**91**
Useful Addresses **91**
Recommended Reading **91**
Glossary **92**
Index **93**

Maps
Fiji Islands **IFC-1**
Fiji and Environs.....................................**2**
Fiji: Day 1 and 2.....................................**22**
Nadi to Suva **26**
Suva...**30**
Natadola...**32**
Nausori Highlands **34**
Navua River and Village Stay **41**
Blue Lagoon Cruise **48**
Viti Levu Hike...**52**
North Fiji...**56**

Following pages:
smiling Fijian youngsters

HISTORY

$\mathbf{F}$iji's human history began some-time around the year 1500BC. There is no evidence as to who those first settlers were. Items unearthed in burial sites and archaeological excavations show that they were of the same stock as those who later became the Polynesians of Tonga, Samoa and the major islands of the east: Tahiti, Hawaii, the Marquesas, Tuamotus, Gambiers, Austral Islands, Easter Island and New Zealand.

Various theories postulate that the first settlers lived in Fiji for more than 1,000 years after its discovery, co-existing with later migrants in a state of war and peace. During this process, the people we recognise today as Polynesian, gradually moved to eastern Fiji, the Lau Islands and Tonga until finally the Fijians as we know them today became dominant over the entire group of islands.

Point of Origin

The undoubted point of origin was Southeast Asia which includes Indonesia, the Philippines, Borneo and Papua New Guinea. Human habitation of New Guinea has now been established to have occurred more than 40,000 years ago. At a later date, new migrants began to move down and at some point, now thought to have been 5,000 years ago, a maritime culture established itself in New Ireland and New Britain and then quickly moved down through the Solomon Islands to Vanuatu, New Caledonia, Fiji and from Fiji to Tonga, Samoa, the Marquesas, Tahiti, Hawaii and New Zealand. This achievement ranks them as the greatest sailors the world has ever known.

Those early sailors who fearlessly roamed the Pacific Ocean are

A typical Fijian bure

Early bare-breasted Fijian beauties

known today as the 'Lapita' people because of a distinct style of pottery first discovered in 1952 at a site in New Caledonia of the same name. Pottery remains discovered in Marquesas tell an interesting story: the material used for grouting came from the Rewa River delta on the island of Viti Levu, in Fiji. This points to a trading contact between the people of Tonga and Fiji and to active voyaging from Tonga to Samoa and the east.

Scientists working with the tools of archaeology, linguistics and botany are still trying to piece together what might really have happened but enough has been revealed for a comprehensive outline. The 'Lapita' people discover and settle Fiji some time before 1500BC. Within a short time of their settlement some continue with exploratory voyages to Tonga, Samoa and then the major islands of east Polynesia. The remaining population increases and war once again becomes endemic. New migrants arrive from the west and human bones are discovered in middens along with those of animals and other foodstuffs. Cannibalism becomes part of life. Fiji enters a period of intense political rivalry which exists up to the time of European contact. Some aspects of Melanesian culture are retained but the material and social culture is principally Polynesian.

European Contact

In 1643, Dutch navigator, Abel Tasman sailed to the north-east of Fiji. The reef which was nearly his ruin, bears the name Heemskirk after one of his ships. Tasman sighted the islands of Taveuni, Qamea, Laucala, Rabi and part of Vanua Levu, but he did not pause to examine his discovery. Captain James Cook was next in 1774. He too láid off the island of Vatoa in southern Lau, left some trinkets ashore and continued to the west without realising the extent of the archipelago.

It was Captain William Bligh who gauged the true extent of Fiji when he sailed through the entire group in 1789 after being set adrift in Tonga by the mutineers who seized HMS *Bounty*. Bligh passed through a portion of Lau in eastern Fiji and then between Koro and Wakaya; within easy distance of Ovalau and through the Vatu i Ra channel which divides Viti Levu from Vanua Levu. He went on past Yasawa i Rara at the north-western extremity, thus

Fijian outrigger canoe

Bau: a once powerful state in Fiji

leaving Fiji behind. A large canoe was launched by the Fijians in pursuit from Yasawa i Rara and came within bow shot of Bligh and his men. Several arrows were fired but Bligh and his men managed to escape. The large, reef-strewn body of water between the north-western coast of Viti Levu, the Yasawa Islands and the Mamanutha Islands is to this day known as Bligh Water.

Cannibals

Europeans who ventured to Fiji before the turn of the century confirmed stories told in Tonga of hazardous reefs and the duplicity of the people and their cannibal appetite. In 1794, the captain of the American brig, *Arthur*, had to defend his ship with musket and cannon. During the course of the next 50 years, less cautious captains would lose theirs. These hazards were sufficient to deter casual traffic, but when sandalwood was discovered it offered sufficient incentive to overlook both the dangers. This period in Fiji's history began just after the turn of the century and ended some 10 years later but it was to have a profound effect on the Fijian people, their culture and politics.

The most important effect was the introduction of the gun and its unscrupulous use by shipwrecked mercenaries, the most significant of whom was Charlie Savage, a Swede. Coupled with the policy of an ambitious chief on the small island of Bau, the weapons proved decisive in war and helped elevate Bau to a state of pre-eminence which it enjoys to this day.

Savage was rewarded with many wives from well-born families; the male issue of which were strangled at birth so as not to complicate future succession claims. He was regarded with dread and awe by most Fijians. His reputation, however, was not sufficient to save his life during a skirmish in Vanua Levu following a dispute. Savage, who went to parley with the opposing side, was taken, drowned by having his head immersed in a pool of water and then dismembered, cooked and eaten before the eyes of his friends. The episode had a happy ending for them. They managed to seize the head priest as hostage and were thus able to get to safety.

Levuka – the old capital in the 19th century

New Trade

Ten years after the demise of the sandalwood trade, a new trade began for *beche de mer* in the 1820s. As with sandalwood, a fortune could be made and this was enough to bring many ships to Fiji where they became embroiled in local conflicts. By now Fiji also had a resident population of European beachcombers. Some like Charlie Savage were shipwrecked castaways; others had jumped ship; some like William Lockerby and David Whippy had been left on the beach because of conflict with their superior officers. Yet others came to seek their fortunes in trade and land speculation.

The natural centre for these men was Levuka, on the island of Ovalau, where the prevailing east-south-east wind made it easy for sailing ships to enter and leave port. Levuka was also in close proximity to the centres of power at Bau and Rewa and the most populous part of Fiji. Some of these men gained fortunes. The American, David Whippy, whose descendants number more than 1,000 today, is a good example. Left ashore by his elder brother, he at first became a mercenary, rose to be trusted ambassador to the state of Bau and later became appointed the American consul for Fiji. Later, he acquired 9,000 acres of land at Wainunu in Vanua Levu, and established a shipyard (which was operated until two years ago by his descendants) and died an honoured man.

At the time of European contact, the relatively new state of Bau was on the ascendant against its neighbours, the ancient and most powerful state of Verata and Rewa. Cakaudrove, which controlled a large part of Vanua Levu, Taveuni and its associated smaller islands, was also in contention but eventually as did the others, acknowledged Bau as pre-eminent.

Tongan Influence

A new consideration was the arrival in Fiji in 1840 of Ma'afu, a Tongan chief who came close to winning control of the entire group. He was thwarted in his ambition by the cession of Fiji to Britain by leading chiefs in 1874. The importance of Wesleyan missionaries who arrived in 1835 from Tonga cannot be overlooked in this equation because it was the conversion in 1853 of Seru Cakobau, Vunivalu of Bau, and decisive Tongan intervention in a war between Cakobau and others, which finally ended the chapter on old Fiji. Cakobau's conversion to Christianity brought about the conversion of most of the population.

Cession to Britain

The inability of Cakobau to form an effective government in the 1870s caused a crisis of a magnitude which could not be resolved. The ever more threatening Tongan presence, directed by the able Ma'afu, poised to swallow Fiji as a colony of Tonga, gave added impetus for the Bauan chief and other leading chiefs, to cede the islands to Great Britain in 1874.

The cession of Fiji encouraged a new wave of European settlers. A plantation society which grew and processed coconuts into oil was developed in the 1840s and began to thrive. Only the lack of cheap, reliable labour held it in check. A stop had been put to 'black birding' prior to cession. This was nothing short of slavery. Islanders in the Solomons and Vanuatu were lured aboard 'recruiting' ships with promises of trade goods and then abducted to be contracted to plantation owners in Fiji.

The planting and processing of sugar cane made it imperative to have a large supply of cheap labour and the colonial administration made the decision to recruit indentured labour from India on five-year contracts. The first contingent arrived in 1878 and the system was to continue until 1916. By this time Fiji's sugar industry was controlled by the Australian Colonial Sugar Refining Company. The company could not survive without the Indians. A government decision allowed those who wished to stay in Fiji to do so despite protests from the Great Council of (Fijian) Chiefs. Most chose to remain and by 1970, when Fiji became independent, Indians outnumbered native Fijians in a total population of over 700,000.

Ratu Seru Cakabau

Military Coups

In 1987, a coalition between Indians and Fijians won the general election and provoked two (bloodless) military coups by the army which was almost entirely composed of Fijian troops. A new constitution was promulgated and

17

Ritual exchange of food and gifts

gave Fijians a guaranteed majority in government. In 1992, five years after the coups, a general election was held. The man who had engineered the coups, Major General Sitiveni Rabuka, became the Prime Minister of a coalition comprising members of his own Fijian party sponsored by the chiefs and that of the general electors who represented people of European, part-European, Chinese, part-Chinese and of Pacific Island origin. Two parties representing the Indian community formed the opposition and have been agitating for a review of the constitution which divides the electorate on racial grounds. It has been agreed a review will take place.

Fijian Culture

The essential nature of Fijian culture survives to this day, due as much to its strengths as to the relative isolation until recently from the rest of the world.

Ninety percent of Fijians still live in villages in the countryside and the power of the *vanua* – one's land and family ties – is still the most powerful cultural force. Extended family units known as *matagali* comprise village communities and own land in common. The concept of individual ownership is foreign in a village where everything is shared and the word *kerekere* means a request that cannot be denied.

However, Fijians who live in cities and are faced with expenditure for rent, food and clothing, find it difficult to cope with requests from relatives who will arrive, expect to be housed, fed and clothed without concern as to who will pay for it all. The problem is magnified when a Fijian ventures into business. If he has a store and a distant relative without money wants to buy something, he cannot refuse, knowing fully well the account will never be settled.

Each village has a chief who in turn owes allegiance to a higher chief. Paramount chiefs represent former political states and command the highest respect. They comprise the Bose Levu Vaka Turaga (The Great Council of Chiefs) whose deliberations and decisions are held by some to be more important than those of parliament. These are men descended from the chiefs who ceded Fiji to Britain in 1874, and who now claim the right of their ancestors to supreme authority in independent Fiji.

The other half of Fiji's population comprises the descendants of Indian indentured labourers who began arriving in the country in 1878. By scraping and saving, by hard work and investment, some have prospered beyond belief. This is a sore point with the Fijians. Thus, they want to maintain political control until such time as they have reached economic parity, a concept which many consider impossible to achieve without a cultural revolution.

Historical Highlights

1736BC Revealed by archaeology as the earliest settlement date.

1643 Abel Tasman sights northeastern islands of Taveuni. Ships *Heemskercq* and *Zeehaen* strike and cross Heemskirk Reef with only slight damage.

1774 James Cook sights and lands at Vatoa Island in southern Lau.

1789 William Bligh sails through the islands in ship's launch after the mutiny on HMS *Bounty* in Tonga.

1792 Bligh returns in the vessel, HMS *Providence*.

1797 The London Missionary Society's ship *Duff* enters Fiji from the north and strikes Heemskirk Reef.

1799 American merchant ship *Ann* and *Hope* sail through Fiji.

1800 American schooner *Argo* wrecked in Lau. Surviving crew bring a devastating epidemic which kills thousands of Fijians.

1804 Olive Slater discovers sandalwood in Vanua Levu and is responsible for the sandalwood trade until the logs are depleted in 1814 which brings about great changes in Fiji.

1820 Marks the start of the *beche de mer* trade of cured sea slugs dominated by American ships from Salem, New England.

1820-1860 British and Yankee ships hunt sperm and humpback whales in Fiji waters and often sign on Fijians as crew.

1825 London Missionary Society attempts to establish mission but catechists remain in Tonga.

1830 Second attempt to set up mission fails after three Tahitian catechists are given hostile reception.

1835 Wesleyan Missionaries David Cargill and William Cross arrive from Tonga and establish at Lau.

1865 First attempt to form a Fiji confederacy as an experiment in a unified government fails

1867 The Tongan Chief, Ma'afu, forms Northern Confederacy with some success.

1870 'Black birding', the kidnapping of people from other South Pacific Islands for cheap labour in Fiji, brought to an end.

1871 Ratu Seru Cakobau, Vunivalu of Bau, declares himself the Tui Viti (King of Fiji) and forms a government at Levuka which survives for three years. Start of the Colo wars.

1874 Fiji ceded to Britain. Measles epidemic begins and eventually claims 40,000 Fijian lives.

1877 Suva is the new capital.

1879 Indentured labour introduced from the India to provide labour on plantations.

1880 Development of sugar cane growing and processing industry.

1881 Rotuma becomes part of the Colony of Fiji.

1888 Birth of Ratu Sir Lala Sukuna, high chief, scholar, soldier of distinction in the 1914 Great War. Ratu Sukuna awarded Medaille Militaire for bravery while serving with the French Foreign Legion on the Western Front.

1919 Indenture system ends officially. Most Indians decide to remain in the Fiji islands.

1928 Kingsford Smith arrives from Hawaii and lands at Albert Park on epic transpacific flight.

1932 Gold discovered at Mt Kasi, Savusavu and Tavua, in Viti Levu, where it is still mined today.

1939 World War II.

1942 Japanese occupy Banaba (Ocean Island); Fijians enlist and serve with distinction with Allied forces in the Solomon Islands.

1952 Fijian troops leave for anti-communist campaign in Malaysia.

1958 Death of Ratu Sir Lala Sukuna.

1970 Fiji becomes independent after 96 years of British rule.

1987 Two military coups against a coalition Government of Fijians and Indians. Formation of interim administration.

1992 General elections under a new constitution which guarantees ethnic Fijians a majority of seats in the Upper and Lower Houses of Parliament. Prime Minister announces that the constitution will be reviewed by a bipartisan commission.

Day itin

$\mathbf{F}$iji's 300 islands do not lend themselves to a quick and breezy visit. Many visitors are happy to be disposed by their travel agent to some island resort which offers dazzling white sand beaches beneath coconut palms and a lagoon of pastel greens, turquoises and deep blues. But for intrepid explorers who want to pack in as much as possible within the space of their holiday, Fiji has much to offer and I have attempted to sign-post what I believe will not be only most enjoyable, but also the best value for money.

The islands of Viti Levu and Vanua Levu comprise more than 80 percent of the land mass. The International Airport is situated at Nadi on the western side of Viti Levu, which is the largest of the group. The airport is situated on the sunny 'dry' side of the island, within close proximity to the popular Yasawa and Mamanutha islands and the Coral Coast.

The Nadi area is where most of Fiji's resorts and hotels are situated and the itineraries assume the visitor will spend at least the first few days here, especially if in Fiji for a short stay. But you could also choose to stay anywhere else on Viti Levu, or the surrounding islands for that matter, and still use the itineraries I've suggested.

Picture postcard beaches

The three day itineraries which include a cruise to the Mamanutha islands and two land tours which span from the east to the southern coast and the westerly capital of Suva are a wonderful introduction to Fiji as they take in the many diverse attractions of this island. *Day 3* gives you the option of spending the night at Suva.

Day Cruise to Mamanutha Islands

There is no finer introduction to Fiji than a cruise from Nadi to the scattered island jewels of the nearby Mamanutha group. This is also a wonderful way to get over jet lag.

Several cruises leave each morning and return late in the afternoon. Buses pick up guests from hotels in the **Nadi** area and from the various resorts on the **Coral Coast** and deposit their eager cargo on the beach ready for a transfer to the cruise of their choice.

The prices vary but most of the cruises are between F$50 and F$74 for the day, inclusive of lunch. For those wanting to strike out on their own, it is possible to hire a 'water taxi' for a day of island-hopping at your own pace. The price depends on the craft chosen, but can be as low as F$229 or as high as F$1,200 for the whole day.

For those prepared to pay more than double the going rate and enjoy the company of a limited number of guests, I would recommend a cruise on the schooner-rigged motor yacht, *Whale's Tale*. This is truly a sybaritic experience which begins the moment you board this magnificent 30-m (98½-ft) luxury yacht at

A cruise on board the Whale's Tale

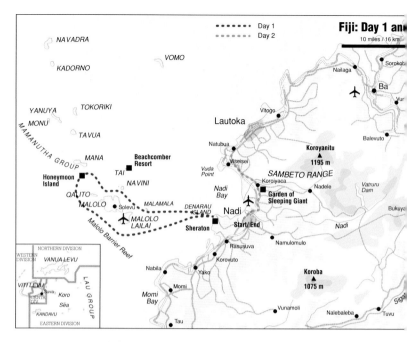

9.45am and find a champagne breakfast awaiting your arrival. The breakfast, a sumptuous luncheon, and all beverages including beer, spirits, wines and snorkelling equipment are included in the price.

The anchor weighed, halyards pulled tight to set the sails, course set for Honeymoon Island, the adventure begins! *Whale's Tale* passes the islands of **Malamala**, **Navini**, **Malolo Lailai** and **Malolo** before reaching its own exclusive destination – **Honeymoon Island**.

There is a magnificent beach and the island is fringed with a live coral reef ideal for snorkelling. There is time to explore the island and the reef before lunch is served on board.

The return voyage in the afternoon takes an alternative route around **Castaway Island**, and the south-western side of Malolo and Malolo Lailai islands, passing a number of resorts on the way and making an additional stop should time permit.

Whale's Tale returns to its anchorage just before sunset. There is still time for guests to enjoy entertainment and cocktails on the poop deck while viewing the sunset and the torch-lighting ceremony on Denarau Island beach. The rate for adults is F$155 inclusive of pick-up from hotels in the Nadi area.

See the hotel tour desk for information on all cruises available and confirm the current rate. You can book the *Whale's Tale* directly at 722455 or 723590 or through the tour desk at your hotel.

There are at least eight other day cruises available from the Nadi-Lautoka area. If the *Whale's Tale* is not available

Aerial view of Malolo Lailai

because it has been fully booked, or because of budget considerations or you are already on an island resort, there are other cruise options to choose from.

South Sea Cruises Limited operates day cruises, half-day cruises, sightseeing cruises, semi-submersible reef-viewing cruises and guest transfers to the various resorts in the Mamanutha Islands.

The company operates a 25-m (82-ft), 300-passenger motor-catamaran twice daily on a regular passenger run. Day trips to Malolo Lailai and Mana Island are offered as part of this service. The day trippers are left ashore in the morning run and picked up in the afternoon. There is time for swimming, snorkelling and various water sports. The company also operates a 34-m (95½-ft), 120-passenger, schooner-rigged motor sailer *Seaspray*, for day and half-day cruises. Call South Sea Cruises direct at 722988/700144 or Fax: 790346 or book through the hotel tour desk.

DAY 2

Sleeping Giant and Viseisei Village

A leisurely day that starts with a visit to the Garden of the Sleeping Giant with its orchids galore. The Viseisei Village is next where you get a glimpse of Fijian village life. If time permits, a visit to the sugar town of Lautoka.

A visit to the **Garden of the Sleeping Giant** will yield something for everyone. For orchid lovers it is like going to heaven. For others it is an experience they seldom forget. Even those who do not care about flowers are struck by its beauty when they leave.

The garden occupies 20ha (50 acres) of gently sloping land at the base of the **Sabeto Range** and takes its name from the outline of a giant who appears to be asleep on top of the mountains. Allow a 25-minute drive from the Nadi area towards Lautoka. Drive past the airport and when you have covered 4.7km (3 miles) you will arrive at the **Wailoko Road** turn-off. Look for a sign on a lamp post on the right-hand side and then turn right into Wailoko Road. Drive another 1.7km (1.1 miles) to the entrance of the Garden of the Sleeping Giant – a verdant greenscape of bush, trees, ponds and more than 150,000 orchids comprising some 1,200 species, 30 of which are native.

The garden has an interesting history. It was started by the American actor, Raymond Burr with the intention of developing

A profusion of orchids

his own collection of orchids. At that time Burr owned Naitauba Island in Lau – one of the prettiest in Fiji. When he decided to move, he sold his island to a religious sect and transferred the orchid garden to a company in which he remains a shareholder. Since then, the garden, destroyed by a number of hurricanes, has had to be replanted anew.

An attractive reception centre in the style of a Fijian *bure* (traditional thatched hut) with a verandah facing down the valley, has comfortable cane furniture. The admission fee includes a cool drink of fruit juice. You can sit and admire the view and then either stroll through the gardens yourself or accompany a guide for an informative tour.

There are orchids everywhere: in the reception area and around it, inside and outside shade houses, on the side of moss-covered banks, and on trees and tree ferns.

Blooms of every shade and size from rich fat hybrids to tiny little natives assail the senses. A long walk through one shade house leads to a pond of water lilies, a bridge and a rest area and then continues through jungle interplanted with flowering trees and shrubs. There are seats where you can relax and absorb what you have seen. Open from 9am–5pm.

Allow 10 minutes comfortable driving time from the garden to **Viseisei Village** while continuing on the way to Lautoka. Legends say that the ancestors of today's Fijians first arrived at **Vuda Point** nearby. The fact that the Chief of Viseisei, Ratu Sir Josaia Tavagia, is the **Tui Vuda** and is one of the two vice-presidents of Fiji suggests the importance of the Vuda *matanitu* (state) in Fijian politics. In pre-European times, several parts of Fiji were recognised as *matanitu* – political confederations which owed allegiance to a paramount chief usually styled *tui*, the title incorporating the name of the area represented. Thus the Tui Vuda is the head of the former 'state' of Vuda.

It is also of interest to know that the village was the home of the former late Prime Minister, Dr Timoci Bavadra, who was deposed in a military coup in 1987. An imposing *bure* was built for Dr Bavadra and is now very popular as a photographic subject.

The village is on the main road and you will know you have arrived because of the

The Tui Vuda (right) of Viseisei Village

Bird's eye view of Viseisei Village

humps on the main highway. These were built to slow traffic due to the number of fatal accidents that used to occur here.

The village has been open to the public for more than 20 years so there is no reason to feel you are intruding or disrupting the villagers' daily routine. People will offer to show visitors around the village and it is appropriate to give a small gratuity to your guide before leaving. The merit of the visit is not so much in seeing the village itself but for the opportunity of meeting local people on their own turf and seeing something of their way of life.

A large Wesleyan church with a memorial commemorating the centenary of the arrival of missionaries in Fiji in 1835 is a point of interest and so is the *bure* of the Tui Vuda.

It is now time to return to Nadi for lunch (see *Eating Out*) and then an afternoon of shopping or relaxing on the beach. Alternatively, continue onto **Lautoka** for a curry lunch at **City Takeaways** at 15 Malau Place or Chinese food at the **Great Wall of China** at 21 Naviti Street.

Lautoka town owes its existence to a large sugar mill (said to be the biggest in the Southern Hemisphere) and a deep water port. It may be of interest to note that Fiji produces some of the world's best sugar.

Lautoka is Fiji's second largest city, but it is small by world standards. The population is only 30,000. The sugar cane railway runs through the centre of the town between a line of tall royal palm trees. From here, the southern **Yasawa Islands** are clearly visible offshore.

For those who do not wish to hire a car and drive, **United Touring Company** will arrange to pick up guests at the various hotels for a half-day tour to the Garden of the Sleeping Giant and Viseisei Village. Check with the hotel tour desk or make a booking direct at 722811.

Nadi to Suva

Travel to the charming capital city of Suva via Queen's Road; driving past sugar cane fields, forests of lush Caribbean pine trees, past the township of Sigatoka, the resorts on the Coral Coast, the community at Pacific Harbour and the Orchid Island Cultural Centre.

It is 197km (122 miles) from Nadi to Suva. This journey will require up to three hours of driving with stops for photography on the way. Allow an extra half-hour to visit the Orchid Island cultural centre just outside Suva. This will time your arrival in Suva for lunch. Those wishing to avoid the long drive back should plan more stops along the way, arrive early evening and spend the night at Suva.

Coral Coast spans from Nadi to Suva

The alternative is to book with **United Touring** for their Suva day trip in an air-conditioned coach complete with a guide. Call United Touring at 722811 or book through the hotel tour desk.

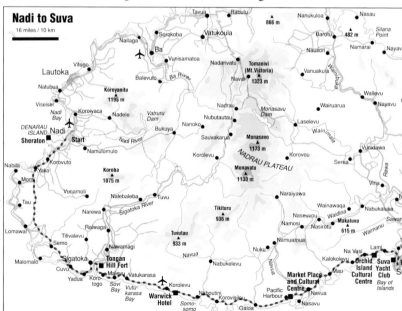

Nadi to Suva

16 miles / 10 km

Because of the distance and the spectacular scenery on the way, a self-drive day trip to Suva should begin early in the morning. An 8am start is ideal. The road is well maintained and is tar-sealed all the way. The only hazards are incompetent drivers who overtake at blind corners and stop abruptly on the road without pulling to the side; and horses and cattle, which, unrestrained by fences, tend to wander as and where they please. Allow an hour or so to reach the town of **Sigatoka**.

Sigatoka is a pleasant little town on the banks of Fiji's second largest river and benefits both from the farming community and the Coral Coast tourist resorts. The site of a former **Tongan fort** on the southern side of the river has been opened and is worth a visit. To get there, cross the bridge and turn right. It is only 4km (2½ miles) from the turn-off.

Seven kilometres (4¼ miles) past the bridge is the village of **Korotogo**, where the highway joins the **Coral Coast**. From here the next 35km (21¾ miles) runs beside the lagoon and through a series of villages and resorts. **Korotogo** marks the southern boundary of the sugar cane growing area. The landscape begins to change as you head towards the south-east. The prevailing trade winds

View of Korotogo resorts

carry moisture and dump it on this coast. The vegetation is lush and the rainforest stretches over hills and mountains as far as the eye can see. Six places offer accommodation in the Korotogo area, including a resort hotel and other more intimate places designed to cater for every type of budget and taste.

The next village is **Malevu** with speed bumps to slow traffic. The road skirts around **Bulu Bay** and then goes round the bigger, open **Sovi Bay**. The southern side of Sovi Bay is popular with locals. It offers safe swimming away from the crashing surf which at times sweeps into the bay. There are parking places on the side of the road. This is definitely a good spot for a break and a swim and, if you left late rather than early, a picnic lunch after the swim.

Next is the village of **Vatukarasa**. It is laid out in the old pattern with a handsome chief's *bure* next to the road as you first enter the village, a wide village green with houses and *bures* on each side and a church at the other end. The opening into Vatukarasa Bay is wide and at times allows a big swell to roll in and crash onto the beach. You pass the resorts of **Tabua Sands**, the **Hide-**

away and **Naviti**, each tucked away among flowers and coconut trees next to its own beach and then reach **Korolevu**, the site of Fiji's first beach resort. The resort closed some years ago but the property was purchased recently by a new company intent on redevelopment that will include a championship golf course, marina, holiday villas and a five-star resort. At the other end of the bay is the **Warwick of Fiji**, formally the Hyatt Regency resort.

The stretch of road between **Korotogo** and **Naboutini** is particularly attractive. It winds around bays, climbs low ridges for views of villages and lagoon, through avenues of tall coconut palms, past rainforest and then moves away from the coast, climbs a series of low hills and emerges on the coast to briefly join the sea again before reaching the wide expanse of open, flat land at **Pacific Harbour**. The islands of **Yanuca** and **Beqa** are visible offshore.

Pacific Harbour was one of Fiji's most ambitious projects. Several hundred acres of lowland were cleared and drained. Lakes were formed and the surrounding land was subdivided and sold. An 18-hole championship golf course designed by Robert Trent Jones Jr and a sumptuous clubhouse was built. A new hotel was constructed beside the beach which is probably the longest in Fiji. A cultural and shopping centre was built around one of the lakes. Investors purchased land, built attractive villas and settled down to a good life which continues to this day. However, the project never realised its potential because the location is prone to a great deal of rain throughout the year and is discouraging to those who want sunshine. It is perfect, though, for those who like gardening.

The **Market Place** and **Cultural Centre,** built around a waterway, is an ideal place for another break. There are curio shops and

restaurants and regular tours are conducted on the waterway to watch Fijian actors demonstrate ancient rituals as well as entertainment programmes.

From Pacific Harbour the road runs through a widening plain, the monotony broken by huge Banyan trees some of which must take up a quarter acre, with dairy and beef cattle, maize, sorghum and rice paddies flourishing over the wide expanse of fertile land. The

Pacific Harbour

township of **Navua** is on the eastern bank of the river where the land is held in small holdings by Indian farmers who specialise in rice cultivation.

The next point of interest is the **Orchid Island** cultural centre on the outskirts of Suva. A billboard and a large double-hulled canoe which was built in the Lau Islands and sailed to the city, mark the turn off to the centre. This is one of Fiji's most popular attractions

Mongoose from Orchid Island

and offers something for everyone. A model Fijian village shows the different regional styles of *bure* construction and a replica of the old-style temple, the *bure kalou,* which is so valued that its likeness is used on the Fiji $20 note.

Visitors are conducted through a chief's *bure* which shows how people lived in pre-European times. On display are weapons, cooking utensils and sleeping arrangements. There are demonstrations of basket and mat weaving, how to make bone fish hooks, pottery, fish and crab traps and various other items.

A covered walkway leads the visitor past Fiji's fauna: the rare and unique Fiji banded iguana, birds, mongooses, flying foxes, a harmless snake, turtles and some of the introduced animals, including monkeys – the only ones in Fiji. A pictorial display illustrates myths and legends and aspects of history, including a gruesome chapter on cannibalism. There are orchids, wild ginger blooms and a path through rainforest. The centre opens from 8am to 4pm. Tel: 361128. Fax: 361064.

Four kilometres (2½ miles) from the centre of Suva is the **Bay of Islands** and the attractive suburb of **Lami**. The **Tradewinds Hotel** sits on the water's edge; yachts and pleasure craft are moored in the bay in the lee of three islands, and there is a convention centre beside the lagoon. From here it is 3km (1¼ miles) to the heart of the city, passing through the **Walu Bay** industrial area and the **Royal Suva Yacht Club**.

Different styles of bures, Orchid Island

You can either opt to spend the night at **Suva** and tour the colourful town the following morning (See Itinerary 1, *Pick & Mix* section) or if you arrive early, tour Suva and then drive back to Nadi. The **Suva Travelodge** along **Victoria Parade** is a comfortable walk from the city centre and an excellent base. It is also within a short distance of major nightclubs and the **Thurston Gardens** and **National Museum**. The **Red Lion** complex, which includes three restaurants and two nightclubs, is the most popular with visitors as are the **Golden Dragon** and **Traps** bars.

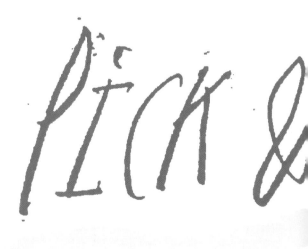

1. Suva

A half-day tour of the capital city of Suva. Take in the city sights and revel in this melting pot of a dozen different races.

Begin your walking tour with **Thurston Gardens** and the **Fiji Museum**. Established in 1904, the museum is a gem. It holds the most comprehensive collection of Fijian artifacts in existence as well as historical collections and artifacts from other Pacific Islands. A double-hulled canoe, built at the turn of the century, commands the main hall. It may be of interest to know that it was used in the making of the movie *His Majesty O'Keefe*, starring Burt Lancaster.

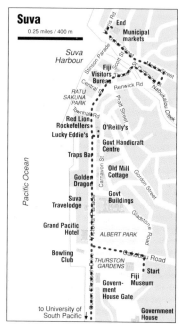

The **Thurston Gardens** houses a large and interesting collection of flora from the South Pacific.

Return to **Victoria Parade** and turn left into **Queen Elizabeth Drive**. This brings you to the gates of **Government House**, the residence of the President of Fiji. A guard in red tunic and white *sulu* at the gate is a favourite photographic subject. If you continue beside the sea, you will reach the **University of the South Pacific** campus, built on a former seaplane base. The hangar is still a dominating feature. The base played a critical role in the war in the Pacific against invading Japanese by mounting long-range reconnaissance missions and mercy flights which saved many lives. The national sports stadium is also located here.

Soldier at the Government House

Retrace your steps up Queen Elizabeth Drive, into the main drag of Victoria Parade, past Thurston Gardens and **Albert Park** on your right and **Suva Bowling Club** and the **Travelodge** on your left. Turn right into **McArthur Street** opposite **O'Reilly's Brasserie** and allow two hours to explore the heart of the city's commercial section. The **Government Handicraft Centre** – which sells a range of Fijian handicrafts including replicas of old weapons, bowls, basketware and *masi* cloth items – is well worth a visit.

Retrace your steps to Victoria Parade, turn right and continue to the north. At the end of the block, cross **Town Hall Road**. **Ratu Sukuna Park** is on the left. **Renwick Road** joins **Victoria Parade** at the triangle with an old *ivi* (native chestnut) tree at its apex with seats at its base.

Much of old Suva still survives in Renwick Road. Victoria Parade joins **Thomson Street** where the old vies with the new, crosses **Nabukalou Creek** and turns into **Cumming Street** which in turn joins **Renwick Road**. Fijian women sell handicrafts under the flamboyant tree on the corner of Thomson and Cumming streets and duty-free dealers crowd each other here, the oldest unchanged part of Suva.

Stroll up Cumming Street, turn left into Renwick Road and then turn left again into **Marks Street** which will bring you down to the **Thomson Street** junction. Continue down towards **Usher Street** to the **Municipal Market**, being careful to avoid sword sellers and 'guides' who will offer to show you around and take you to the places where you will get the 'best deal'.

The Municipal Market and adjoining bus-stand cover an

Clock tower, Thurston Gardens

entire city block and offer a fascinating glimpse of Fiji's multiracial community. The best days are Friday and Saturday mornings, but the markets may be crowded to the point where it is difficult to get through. All the products of land, lagoon and ocean are on display. From the markets follow **Stinson Parade** along the foreshore, past Ratu Sukuna Park and eventually back to the main drag of Victoria Parade. Have lunch at the O'Reilley's Brasserie, just before the McArthur Street turning, or at the **Old Mill Cottage** further down at **Carnavon Street**.

2. Natadola Beach Picnic and Coral Coast Railway

See the historic Momi Bay guns; a picnic at Natadola Beach or a ride on the toy train Coral Coast Railway; visit the spectacular Kulukulu sand dunes.

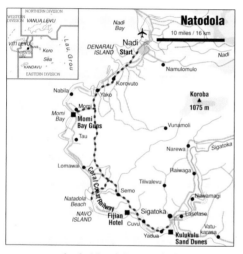

Having packed a picnic lunch, drive on the **Queen's Highway** towards Suva. The first point of interest is 15km (9¼ miles) from town at the Momi Bay turn-off where a sign proclaims a place of historic interest – the site of the **Momi Bay** guns. These are World War II relics restored by the National Trust of Fiji.

Follow the signposts to the location. The guns and the grounds which overlook Momi Bay and the main channel in the barrier reef are not spectacular, but may be of interest to those interested in the Pacific phase of World War II. The Mamanutha Islands are clearly visible and in fact, this is the closest point to the islands. Return again to the main road and continue south towards Suva.

It takes about 25 minutes to reach the Natadola Beach turn-off at **Maro Road**, 40km (25 miles) from Nadi. Maro Road is signposted and the turn-off is easy to find as there is a mosque on the left, a Hindu temple just above the turn-off on the right, and a sign which says '**Tuva Indian School**'. This is still the heart of the sugar cane growing area and the road twists and winds its way to the sea between sugar cane farms and mosques. You cross the river twice and this will confirm you are on the right road. Keep bearing left. Allow 15 minutes for a comfortable drive from the turn-off before arriving at the beach.

There is more than a mile of magnificent white sand curving in

Picturesque Natadola Beach

an arc from **Navo Island** in the south to the north-west. The prevailing tradewind comes off the land so that the extensive bay is usually calm and ideal for windsurfing. Coral reefs encompass the bay to nearly a mile offshore where a wide passage allows safe entry into the bay. Yachtsmen tend to avoid this anchorage because the wide entrance allows a swell from the south to roll into the bay causing boats to rock uncomfortably. The same swell will sometimes produce a low surf ideal for body surfing. The beach is popular with local people who will be found there on weekends picnicking or enjoying barbecues.

Many plans have been made to turn the area into a major tourist attraction with resorts, golf course, marina, shopping centre and condominiums. It says much for the small scale of Fiji's tourist industry that one of the most attractive pieces of real estate has not yet been developed. Coral reefs on each side of the bay offer interesting snorkelling but the main feature is the expanse of white sand.

For a ride of a different kind and a pre-arranged picnic, continue on the main highway for another 15 minutes to the **Coral Coast Railway** terminal at the **Fijian Hotel** turn off. From here, the Coral Coast train departs at 10am and reaches Natadola Beach just before noon. It chugs along the track beside the lagoon, through country impossible to enjoy otherwise because there is no other access. A barbecue lunch is served and there is enough time for swimming, snorkelling and horse riding before the departure at 3pm for the one-hour ride back.

All aboard!

F$60.50 per person.

The Coral Coast train ride is a great family side-show. The railway is part of the network established by the

Colonial Sugar Refining Company as it developed the sugar industry. The trains hauled sugar cane to Lautoka for processing and when the Fiji government purchased the company in 1970, the railway system was maintained. Today, much of the sugar cane is still hauled to Lautoka on this quaint, narrow gauge railway. A New Zealand entrepreneur built period coaches, a terminal station at the Fijian and went into business using the existing infrastructure. The Natadola service runs each day except Monday.

If time permits, continue for another 10km (6¼ miles) to the **Kulukulu sand dunes** – surely one of the most arresting sights in Fiji. The turn-off has a shop and a sign advertising 'Club Masa'. Follow this road to the dunes, park and then ascend the dunes for panoramic views of the sea, the Sigatoka River where it meets the ocean and the dunes. The highest part is no more than 30½m (100 ft) above sea level, but it is spectacular nevertheless.

Some of Fiji's most important archaeological finds were made on these sands. The prevailing wind constantly exposes pottery shards and sometimes human remains. The oldest human remains to have been found in the Fiji-Polynesian part of the Pacific came from the Kulukulu sand dunes. Fresh water from the Sigatoka River has impaired coral growth and as there is no barrier reef, a large surf usually thunders onto the exposed beach. It is the haunt of surfers and windsurfers but only strong swimmers or experienced surfers should venture here.

3. Nausori Highlands

Hire a four-wheel drive car, prepare a picnic lunch, pack swimming gear and set off to explore something of Fiji's wilderness. Make an early start for a full day of adventure. There are two different routes to choose from, both with equally breathtaking and rugged scenery. Do not attempt both itineraries on the same day.

This is a tour for the experienced driver as the roads can be very treacherous. The rental car company will insist on an indemnity clause as some cars have been damaged through careless or incompetent driving.

A 4-wheel drive is a must

Route 1. Allow 15 minutes from Nadi to the Nausori Highlands road turn-off. The easiest way is to drive south (towards Suva) through the town and turn left at the service station. There is a Hindu temple on the opposite side of the road. Follow this road for 4.8km (3 miles) and keep your eyes peeled for the **Nausori Highlands** signpost on your right.

From then on there is virtually

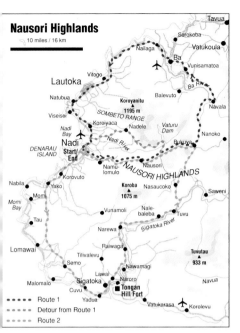

Nausori Highlands

10 miles / 16 km

Tavua
Sorokoba
Vatukoula
Nailaga
Ba
Vunisamatoa
Vitogo
Balevuto
Ba River
Lautoka
Navala
Natubua
Koroyanitu
1195 m
SOMBETO RANGE
Nanoko
Viseisei
Koroiyaca
Nadele
Vaturu Dam
Nadi Bay
Nadi River
Bukuya
Nadi
DENARAU ISLAND
Start/End
Namu-lomulo
Nausori
NAUSORI HIGHLANDS
Korovuto
Nabila
Yako
Koroba
1075 m
Nasaucoko
Saweni
Momi
Momi Bay
Vunamoli
Nale-baleba
Tuvu
Tau
Narewa
Sigatoka River
Raiwaqa
Tuvutau
933 m
Lomawai
Tilivalevu
Semo
Nawamagi
Lawai
Navua
Malomalo
Sigatoka
Naroro
Cuvu
Tongan Hill Fort
Yadua
Vatukarasa
Korolevu

●●●●● Route 1
●●●●● Detour from Route 1
●●●●● Route 2

only one road, 34-km (21-miles) long, to the Bukuya turn-off. It leaves the Nadi flats and begins ascending over rolling country of sugar cane farms towards the highlands. The road then turns steeply uphill and follows a narrow ridge with sharp bends.

Massive volcanic rocks and sheer cliff faces overlooking Nadi town, the airport and the offshore islands offer good photographic subjects.

There is a forestry station and village at **Nausori** when you reach the top. Once the site of a sawmill, it is now the centre of an ambitious replanting programme with Caribbean Pine. The road soon leaves the pine plantations and continues through steep country with rainforest as your company. On the right begins the **Sigatoka River** catchment and the **Nadi River** is on the left. A turn-off to the left marks the access road to **Vaturu Dam**, the source of fresh water for Nadi and Lautoka.

For those wishing a less adventurous trip, turn left to the dam and after a picnic lunch, descend via the **Sabeto Valley** to the main highway north of the airport. Otherwise continue on towards **Bukuya** for another 12km (7½ miles) and turn left before reaching the village. The road now follows the **Ba River** catchment towards

Road between Bukuya and Navala Village

Down the Ba River in a bilibili

the village of **Navala** 17km (10½ miles) from the junction. On the way there are plenty of picturesque spots for a picnic.

Some time ago, the chief and people of Navala made the decision to keep the village traditional and allow only *bures* to be built for housing. As a result Navala is a remarkable village and an ideal subject for photography. The village accepts visitors who may wish to stay the night. The usual courtesies should be followed if you intend to visit. This requires the presentation of a kilogramme of *yaqona* (powdered root of the piper mysthisticum plant) to the *turaga ni koro* (village headman) with the request that you wish to look around the village and take some photographs.

Allow an hour's careful driving from Navala, 18km (11¼ miles), to reach the township of **Ba**. As you descend from Navala, the road passes sugar cane farms and the compounds of Indian farmers and their families. Some of the fields are perched on ledges, offering testimony to the ingenuity of the farmers. On leaving Navala, the Ba River enters a gorge and this is also the site of Fiji's whitewater rafting. The excitement of the ride depends on the volume of the water in the river and for that reason rafting is best after heavy rainfall in the highlands.

The road begins its descent to Ba from a high ridge overlooking the lowlands and the sparkling sea in the distance. Much like the road up to the Nausori Highlands, it is steep and winding until it reaches low ground. The road is tar-sealed some miles before the township and passes the sugar mill on the banks of the river. The town itself is a quaint one-street collection of shops. Turn left to return to Nadi. You will know you are on the right road when you cross a one-way bridge where traffic is regulated by traffic lights which no one seems to take much notice of. The western side of the river has some rather ostentatious houses built by prosperous Indian merchants. It is 72km (44¾ miles) from Ba to Nadi and 38km

(23½ miles) to Lautoka on a tar-sealed highway. Allow 1¼ hours and an extra 15 minutes during the sugar cane harvest season when you may encounter slow-moving trucks carting cane to the mill. The section between Ba and Lautoka offers great views of sugar cane fields, Bligh Water, the Yasawa Islands and pine tree plantations on steep hills.

The distances involved are not great but because of the state of the road, this route, with a stop for a swim and picnic and then a visit to Navala village, will require a whole day.

Route 2. An alternative route, but just as spectacular, is to drive from Nadi onto the **Queen's Highway** to **Sigatoka** town, 77km (48 miles), and from there up the **Sigatoka Valley** road. This will eventually bring you back to Nadi through the Nausori Highlands.

There are many points of interest along this route. The site of a **Tongan Fort** at **Naroro** seen on the opposite side of the river is worth a visit. This necessitates crossing the Sigatoka River via a one-way bridge and turning left at the end of the bridge. It is 4km (2½ miles) to the village. The old fort commanded the Sigatoka River and offers breathtaking views. Return to the Nadi side of the river and turn right up the valley road to the village of **Lawai** where pottery is still made in the time-honoured way.

The bountiful fertility of the **Sigatoka River Valley** has earned it the title of the 'salad bowl' of Fiji. A full range of vegetables thrive in the rich soils here, whilst a government agricultural research station, 6½km (4 miles) from town, is constantly experimenting with new varieties and species.

The road up the valley is not tar-sealed and requires attentive driving. It follows the river for most of the way, climbs two steep ridges offering magnificent scenery. There are villages on the way and 35km (21¾ miles) up the road, tobacco-drying kilns are a distinct landmark at **Nalebaleba**. Seven kilometres (4¼ miles) further, a road on the left leads to Bukuya while the valley road continues to its terminal at Korolevu. Follow the road to Bukuya. There are two villages, both with access roads on the way. The first is **Nasaucoko** which was the headquarters of government troops during the Colo war against the mountain people in 1876, two years after cession of Fiji to Britain. It was here that some of the leading rebels were hanged and the war brought to an end.

It is 17km (10½ miles) from the time you leave the valley

Navala village, Viti Levu

road and reach the village of **Bukuya**. A little way past the village take the turn to the left and this will eventually lead back to Nadi. Allow at least five hours, plus extra time for swimming and picnicking, photography and for making friends along the way, for each of the above excursions.

Alternatively, book with **Highlands Tours**, Tel: 520285, for a day trip to Nasaucoko Village which includes lunch and a visit to the village. Check with your hotel tour desk for more information. The tour covers the same ground as a self-drive excursion up the Sigatoka River Valley, but diverts to Nasaucoko village, where lunch is served and returns by the same route.

4. Levuka: Fiji's Old Capital

There is no question that the town of Levuka, on the island of Ovalau, situated off the western coast of Viti Levu is a special place, not least because of its historical significance. Time seems to stand still here and those who venture beyond the tourist traps will be delightfully surprised with their discovery.

Levuka town, once Fiji's capital, owes its origin to the direction of the prevailing east-south-east tradewinds which allowed sailing ships to enter and leave port without difficulty, to its central position on the island of Ovalau within the Lomaiviti group, and its

proximity to the once politically powerful states of Bau, Verata, Rewa and Cakaudrove. When Fiji became a British possession in 1874, Levuka's days as the capital were numbered.

The town, on Ovalau's southwest coast, sits on a narrow strip of land with a bush-clad mountain directly at its back. It was the lack of available space

Beach Street in sleepy Levuka

which caused the administration to move to Suva and consigned Levuka to its memories. It was also this move which caused Levuka to remain in its time warp. Levuka's main thoroughfare, **Beach Street**, is one of the last unchanged places in the Pacific and various organisations are doing their best to try and keep it this way so it will remain a living museum of Fiji's (and the South Pacific's) colourful past.

The easiest way to get to Levuka is to fly from Nausori Airport near Suva. The 10-minute flight costs just under F$30 one way. If you're planning to do an island hop, Fiji Air also has a special package which allows you to fly from Nadi to Kadavu, Levuka, Savusavu, Taveuni and return for F$180.

The fact that Levuka did not decline is due to a fish cannery operated by the Pacific Fishing Company which buys skipjack tuna

Levuka town on the island of Ovalau

from local and overseas contract fishermen and pumps money into the community through wages and services. The cannery complex is located next to the wharf at the southern end of Beach Street, the town's main (and virtually only) thoroughfare. A stroll around the town will take no more than 20 minutes. This will allow a thorough look at most of the historic landmarks which include the **Catholic Church**, with the cross on the bell tower also serving as one of the lead-in lights into the harbour; **Levuka Public School** which is the oldest in the country; the **Ovalau Club**; the old **Town Hall** just beside the club; the **Masonic Lodge**; the **Royal Hotel** which is the oldest operating hotel in the Pacific (some parts dating from 1860); and the **Totoga Falls**, reached by following a track from the end of Bath Road.

One kilometre south of the cannery is **Nasova** and its commemorative park. This is where Fiji was ceded to Britain in 1874 and where in 1970, Prince Charles on behalf of his mother, Queen Elizabeth II, returned Fiji to the descendants of the chiefs who had given it to Queen Victoria 96 years ago.

As there are four flights to Levuka each day, a visit in the morning, lunch and return will accomplish most of the objectives of the casual traveller. Fiji Air, in association with the National Museum offers a special package day tour for just under F$60 which includes a return flight, morning tea and lunch at Levuka and two guided tours: one around the town and another bush walk up the hill. The tours cost extra. The bush walk ascends to a high point overlooking the town and the adjacent islands. This is definitely one of the best deals on offer in Fiji.

The more adventurous should linger a day or so. The **Royal Hotel** has rates which begin at F$14. The hotel is a pick up point for day trips to two nearby islands and for bush walks. The **Old Continental Inn** has accommodation from F$7 to F$17 including breakfast, and also operates a popular, low budget resort at **Lelu-**

via, a small outlying island where the top rate for a *bure* and meals is F$20 a day. **Mavida Lodge** with rates from F$5 to F$16 per day is one of the best deals in the country. The **Ovalau Resort** is the closest you will find to a tourist resort and accommodation consists of restored whaler's cottages on a copra plantation 3km (1¼ miles) north of the town. Rates from F$20 to F$90.

5. Ba River Run

Whitewater rafting in Fiji depends on the volume of water in the river and this in turn depends on the amount of rain. But regardless of whether or not the amount of water in the river is sufficient to provide a thrilling ride, a day out on the river is still an experience that should not be missed.

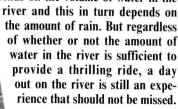

Aerial view of Ba River Valley

When the volume of water is high in the **Ba**, the ride in the inflatable raft is a thrilling one. When the water is low, there is no adrenalin rush. Instead, the raft drifts along over the crystal waters with bush-covered cliffs flanking on each side. There is time to swim and enjoy a picnic lunch surrounded by the raw beauty of Fiji's wilderness.

Each morning at 8.30am the **Roaring Thunder Whitewater Rafting Company** picks up would-be rafters in the Nadi-Lautoka area and then heads towards the town of Ba on the first leg of the journey to the upper reaches of the Ba River. For those who have not already explored this country (see Itinerary 3, *Pick & Mix* section), this is an ideal opportunity to enjoy a delightful scenic drive

An adrenalin-pumping ride down the Ba

through sugar cane fields with views of Bligh Water and the Ya-sawa Islands in the distance.

The road turns south soon after crossing the Ba River at the township and runs through the fertile alluvial lowlands before ascending steeply up the highlands. The higher the ascent, the more spectacular the landscape below. The road then turns inland, winding down towards the river with vistas of mountains at every turn and the steep gorge below. The road crosses the Ba River, ascends over the next ridge and while within easy distance of **Navala Village**, arrives at the starting point of the rafting trip.

The company provides a guide, a crash course on rafting and the necessary equipment: helmet, life vest and lunch with transport to and from the river. Book direct at 780029 or through the hotel tour desk.

6. Navua River Trip

Navua River and Village Stay
10 miles / 16 km

- **••••••** Itinerary 6
- **‑ ‑ ‑ ‑** Optional Stops for Itinerary 7

A river journey up the Navua River, followed by a traditional welcome and lunch at Namuamua Village.

The best way to enjoy this tour is to book with **United Touring Company** either direct or through the hotel tour desk. Tel: 722811. The bus picks up guests from the Nadi hotels from 8am in the morning and along the Coral Coast resorts until it arrives at Navua township on the banks of the **Navua River** about 11.30am. A tour guide offers commentary along the way.

As **Navua town** is only 20 minutes from Suva, the trip covers most of Queen's Highway and offers a spectacular vista of sugar cane fields and pine tree forests, with coastal views that delight with the ever-changing colours of the lagoon glimpsed through tall coconut trees.

But the drive, pleasant as it is, is only an appetiser for the main course – the boat ride up the Navua River to Namuamua village. Navua town itself, which serves the farmers of the river delta, is small and slow. Many of the quaint buildings are of turn-of-the-century vintage. A market-place spills over onto the footpath and the edge of the road.

Among the many flat-bottom, narrow punts at the jetty are some which came down to bring produce to the market that morning and

Punting up the Navua River

will return up river later in the day. One of these will also take visitors to Namuamua Village.

Seated two abreast, hip to hip and thigh to thigh, the boat has only a few inches of freeboard. The pilot cranks the outboard engine, the guide sits for'ed and the voyage begins.

The calm stillness of the river suggests unplumbed depths and it comes as a surprise when the helmsman leaps out, tilts the engine up and walks the punt over a shallow bank.

Forty minutes after leaving Navua, the punt passes the village of **Nakavu**. This is the last village with a road access. The river enters a gorge with bush-clad hills. There are tall tree ferns, vine-clad giants, clumps of bright green, fluffy bamboo and small grassy banks. The river narrows and the punt, like a homing salmon, finds the line of least resistance up frothing rapids. Spectacular waterfalls tumble down cliff faces. Some flash like silver behind a screen of bamboo, others majestic as they gush 30m (98.4ft) to the river.

It takes an additional 40 minutes to reach Namuamua village, but this can vary depending on the size of the engine and the amount of water in the river. If the river is low, it requires man-handling over the shallows, a function performed by the boatmen while the you sit tight. As the punt emerges from the gorge, the country opens a little. **Nukusere** village, high on the bank, is the first major settlement easily noticed because of the raft of colourful river punts moored below. A few hundred metres ahead, on the opposite bank, is **Namuamua**.

School children await your arrival and you are led up into a house where a presentation of *yaqona* is made on your behalf. The *yaqona* served, the guide takes the group on a tour of the village.

After a hearty lunch of chicken, sausage, dalo leaf in coconut cream and boiled cassava, eaten off mats covering the floor, there is a *meke* or communal dance put up by young men. Formal entertainment complete, the band strikes a tune and you're invited to dance. Leaving the village at 3pm, you are back at Navua town at 4pm, the trip on the punt down river taking much less time.

A drink of yaqona… followed by lunch

Right: a waterfall glimpsed on the way up Navua River

EXCURSIONS

7. Namuamua Village Stay

A few days' stay at a village will provide an interesting insight into traditional life, and a chance to experience Fijian hospitality and warmth at its best.

Take the Navua River trip (see Itinerary 6, *Pick & Mix* section). At the end of the visit inform your hosts that you would like to spend a night or two with them. It does not matter that the people have had no prior notification. Just inform your hosts, more particularly **Eremasi Tuicaumia** or **Semesa Caginivalu** and they will organise a family who will act as hosts.

For those wishing to make an advance booking, a call must be booked with the radio operator in Suva at 311010, to the radio telephone at Namuamua village on the call sign 452 RP2. The village operator will then fetch Eremasi or Semesa.

In making your own arrangements, the following should be the rule: Allow F$30–F$40 for the punt voyage from Navua. F$15 should be allocated for each guest per night for accommodation and food. Additional items such as cans of corned beef, rice, sugar, tea and flour should be purchased in Navua to share with your host family. Such items are luxuries for the villagers. The quantity depends on the intended length of stay. An additional F$3 should be allowed for a guide for each day one is required. Those wishing to

Preparing yaqona for the welcome ceremony

use horses (there are no saddles) should budget F$5 a day. The guide will be a villager only too happy to show you around, take you hiking, hunting for wild boar or fish-

Villagers and guests at Namuamua

ing in the river. Take a casting rod as there are large mouth bass to be caught for sport and for your dinner.

Fijian etiquette requires the presentation of *yaqona* to your hosts and the whole village will assemble to accept the offering. A kilogramme of *yaqona* is ample and will cost F$14–F$18 depending on the market rate. The people of Namuamua cultivate *yaqona* so it is best to purchase it at the village and indirectly contribute cash to the village economy.

Many village activities can be experienced without planning. The women can go fishing for prawns and fish; the men can go to plantations or hunt for wild boar. Hiking to nearby villages upstream or to Nukusere downstream requires a guide. There are seven villages upstream. These are **Navuandra**, **Nakavika**, **Navunikambi**, **Saliandrau**, **Naggarawai**, **Wainimakatu** and **Naraiyawa** (see map on page 41). It is possible to make arrangements to stay overnight at these villages also. In the late afternoon there will be a game of touch rugby or volleyball, followed by a bath in the river and then a bowl of *yaqona* and the telling of stories, playing of guitars and songs in the evening. Visitors will be asked many questions. As Fijians will happily answer any question you ask them, they will expect the same of you.

Navua township is also the port of departure for the island of **Beqa**, about 16km (10 miles) offshore. This is the home of the legendary firewalkers who come from the island, more specifically, from the village of **Rukua** which has now opened its doors to visitors in a low key way.

The contact person is **Mikaele Funaki**, of Island and Village Tours, GPO Box 14328, Suva, Tel: 340079 or 391002. A four-day, three-night visit with a host Fijian family, including all meals, road and boat transport to and from the island will cost you about F$100. A longer stay is also possible.

Beqa Island has renowned coral reefs ideal for swimming and snorkelling. It is a wonderful island for hiking and exploring and for getting to know Fijian people on their own terms.

Firewalkers from Rukua, Beqa Island

8. Mamanutha Islands: Beachcomber Resort

No stay in Fiji is quite complete without a stay at one of its many island resorts. Beachcomber Resort in the Mamanutha group has something for everyone.

The great Viti Levu barrier reef sweeps in an arc to the north from Momi to the Yasawa Islands and then continues to the north-western extremity of Vanua Levu at Udu Point.

Sun-drenched beaches

Lying in calm water behind the reef near Momi and within close proximity to the Nadi International Airport, are more than two dozen islands of the **Mamanutha** group. These have long been acknowledged as among some of the most beautiful to be found anywhere on earth and are now the home of 12 island resorts.

Among the first to be developed was **Beachcomber Island**. It was formerly the playground of Fiji-born rancher/butcher Dan Costello. It was his idea of fun to get a boatload of friends on a Friday night, provision adequately with good food and beverages and head for the island to enjoy a weekend of fishing, diving, barbecues and evenings of guitars and songs around a campfire. When the jet age roared into Nadi in the early 1960s, fun-loving flight crews, complete with hostesses, somehow managed to get included.

The inevitable soon happened: Dan Costello took a lease on the island, fitted out an old island trader, named it *Ratu Bulumakau* (Chief Bull), and started daily trips to the island. The one-hour trip included a bar, string band and a great deal of good clean fun. Pretty soon people said: why don't you build a few *bures* so we can stay longer? That's exactly what he did and **Beachcomber Island Resort** was born.

Beachcomber Island is unique among the 12 resorts in the Mamanutha Islands in that it caters to all tastes, from backpackers who can enjoy accommodation in a native-style long house dormitory and all meals for an inclusive price of F$57 per day, to the young at heart who can join the many activities and retire to the privacy of a secluded *bure* where prices are F$165 to F$217 single/double inclusive of all meals.

These days the schooner-rigged *Tui Tai*

Windsurf on transparent waters

sails each day from Lautoka with connecting courtesy coaches to and from Nadi in the morning and the afternoon to the island, bringing guests and day-trippers who come to enjoy the special ambience the island offers as well as activities such as windsurfing, hobie cat sailing, snorkelling, scuba diving, fishing and parasailing. At night there is dancing barefoot on the sand.

The reputation established by Costello is jealously guarded by him to this day and the routine of so many years ago is still maintained religiously.

Each Friday, Costello boards the *Tui Tai* for the island and spends the weekend not so much for making merry as in the past, but to make sure his guests enjoy themselves as all those countless thousands of others have done before them. For more information and bookings call 661500 or Fax: 664496 (Lautoka office).

Idyllic Beachcomber Island Resort

9. Yasawas: The Blue Lagoon Cruise

The Yasawa Islands, lying like a chain of blue beads in the horizon, are reminiscent of the quintessential South Pacific. The Blue Lagoon cruise presents highlights of these islands.

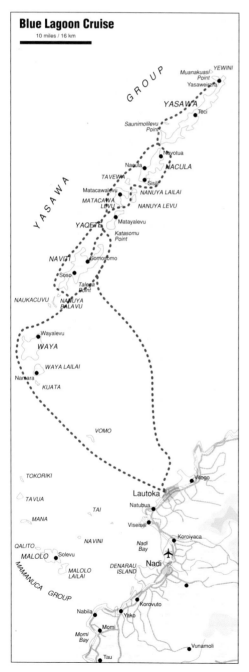

Blue Lagoon Cruise
10 miles / 16 km

The words, 'blue lagoon' are almost a cliche after two Hollywood movies of the same name showed the world a fantasy of two ship-wrecked children cast ashore on a tropical island. Surrounded by nature, they grow to adulthood, find love and happiness and are eventually rescued.

Both movies were shot in Fiji in the **Yasawa Islands**, a group of spectacularly beautiful islands 40km (25 miles) north-west of Lautoka. The first movie, starring Jean Simmons, was filmed in 1948 and the second, less successful remake in 1979, featured Brooke Shields.

A New Zealand naval officer, the late Trever Withers, helped in the 1948 production. He had come to Fiji with the famed aviator, Harold Gatty, to see if there were sufficient tuna in Fijian waters for a major fishery. They spent four years conducting surveys and reluctantly agreed there was not enough fish, though time was to prove them wrong as Fiji now has a major cannery.

Withers fell in love with the Yasawa Islands and their people and set up the **Blue Lagoon Cruise**, borrowing the name from the movie. It seemed like such a good idea at the time, but he never saw it succeed. After more than 15 years of hard struggle,

Jean Simmons, in the original 'Blue Lagoon'

Withers became ill and sold his interest. Over the past 25 years the company has developed an unsurpassed reputation and is considered to be one of Fiji's leading attractions. It is also the only cruise operator to cruise around the Yasawas.

It took that amount of time for the rest of the world to discover the islands and people that Captain Withers had found.

For those who wish to indulge in adventure and love calm, warm waters, exploring exotic islands and beaches, snorkelling, dancing barefoot on the sand or the feel of a teak deck under their feet, indulging in food cooked in an underground *lovos* and visits to native villages, the Blue Lagoon Cruise is an excellent choice.

Cruise vessels depart virtually every day from the port of Lautoka and offer three different cruises: the original four-day, a club cruise of the same duration and a seven-day cruise. The charm of the cruises is the fact that the Yasawa Islands are only a short distance

Crystal clear waters and seafood aplenty in the Yasawas

Coral reefs in the lagoon at Naviti Island, Yasawas

from Lautoka – the closest is **Waya** only 48km (30 miles) away so there is never the feeling of being exposed to the weather in the open sea. The vessels run through colourful coral reefs of the Bligh Water to the Yasawa Islands. There are 10 major islands and a total of 60, including small ones, stretching in line for more than 80km (49¾ miles). The islands are completely undeveloped save for one. The cruise boats weave a magical course between the islands, cruising an average of four hours each day to new destinations. This is usually early in the morning or late in the afternoon so there is ample time on shore.

Fijian entertainment

The cruise vessels are manned by a Fijian crew, many of whom come from the Yasawa Islands. They are perfect hosts; easy and friendly without being obsequious or patronising. The Fijians regard visitors as honoured guests and take pleasure in caring for them.

Accommodation is offered in two or three bedroom air-conditioned cabins each with its own bathroom and toilet. Deck cabins have windows, lower cabins have port-holes. The price includes breakfast, lunch and dinner and morning and afternoon tea with freshly baked cakes. The chefs also bake bread each morning.

There is a varied menu of Fijian, Indian and European dishes, buffets, beach barbecues of unlimited steaks, salads and fruits, island nights where the food is cooked in *lovos*, and traditional Fijian entertainment.

Fares can be as low as F$506 for sharing a B deck triple cabin on the four-day Blue Lagoon 'original' cruise, F$715 for sharing a twin cabin on the A deck or up to F$1,023 for single occupancy in an A deck cabin. The seven-day cruise is priced between F$1,133 for a triple share B deck cabin and F$2,750 for single occupancy of a bridge deck cabin.

The four-day 'club' cruise which offers berths on the new Princess-class boats and other luxurious perks, costs approximately F$200 more for each category of cabin chosen.

Bookings can be made at 661622/661268, Fax: 664098, or through your travel agent.

10. Viti Levu: Interior Hike

There are ample rewards awaiting the adventurer bold enough to leave his air-conditioned room and venture into the rugged interior of Fiji.

In 1970 I took a five-day hike through the interior of **Viti Levu**. My guide at that time was 60-year-old **Ilai Naibose**. We became good friends. I paid his fee and gave him a donation and plenty of advice on how to start his own business. Thus, **Inland Safaris** was born. Ilai is now 82 years of age, but his legs are still strong and on occasions he happily disappears into the bush with a tour party and shows them the 'real' Fiji and the 'real' Fijians.

I have been back in the interior of Viti Levu several times but the memory of that first trip with Ilai is as vivid today as it was when we finished our hike. From **Tavua** town we climbed a zigzag road in an old bus up the face of Fiji's highest mountain range to the forestry settlement at **Nadarivatu** and spent the first cool night at an elevation of more than 607m (2,000ft) above sea level. The next day we followed an ancient trail on mountain ridges, through rainforest and across sparkling mountain streams to Navai, and then onto Nadrau, almost in the very heart of the main island. Early next morning, we set off on the longest hike of the trip – 10 hours of walking to the village of **Nubutautau**.

It was always my ambition to see this village because it is famous

Friendly villagers you will meet on your hike

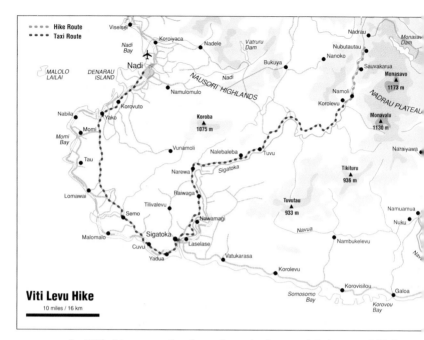

Viti Levu Hike

10 miles / 16 km

in Fiji's history as the place where the Reverend Baker was killed and eaten in 1867 – a time when most other parts of Fiji had accepted Christianity and given up cannibalism. Our first view of the village was through forest giants on a high ridge above the valley.

It was a peaceful settlement of a few *bures*, the village having been moved from a naturally strong position to open ground. We arrived late in the afternoon, in time to be welcomed by the great, great, grandchildren of the chief who ordered Baker killed and were even shown the axe with which the blow was struck.

Many stories are told as to why the missionary was killed and even Jack London wrote of the event, giving the reason as Baker's ignorance of Fijian etiquette. This version of events says that Baker had a comb which he used in the presence of the chief. By all accounts it was a handsome comb of whalebone and the chief asked to see it. He admired it and then put it into his hair, thus in Fijian custom

Interior, Viti Levu

claiming it. Baker, seeing that it was not returned, rose, walked to the chief and took it out of his hair, committing in Fijian eyes the greatest profanity as a chief's head was always held sacred. His fate was sealed.

The most likely cause of his death, however, was political. A whale's tooth (*tabua*) was sent up to Nubutautau by a faction opposed to Christianity. The chief accepted the *tabua* and ordered Baker killed.

I was taken to the spot where Baker fell. A small mound of stones, in the shade of tall bamboo, was the only memorial. Since then, an act of atonement has been performed by the villagers and a small memorial erected. Three days later, we emerged at the **Keyasi** in the **Sigatoka River** valley and took a bus back to the coast.

Though I have done these hikes many times since, I still remember the first time I went for an evening bath in a mountain river accompanied by virtually all the children in the village. I remember the fishing and hunting; going down river in a *bili-bili* bamboo raft; tasty meals which in retrospect seem like feasts – fresh river prawns cooked in *dalo* leaves and coconut cream, wild pork cut into fine slivers and cooked with pumpkin and chilli peppers, broiled fish and chicken soup with mounds of dalo, yams and cassava, and fresh papaya, bananas and pineapple. Above all I remember the quiet, measured pace of village life, the open friendly faces of the people and the peace and tranquillity.

The original stonewash

Ilai Naibose and his Inland Safaris will show you this world or at least a small part of it, depending on how much time you have. He can be contacted through the Fiji Visitors Bureau or directly at 362314 or 362003. He does not go to Nubutautau now as the trip is too demanding for most but on request he will take you there.

The main route Ilai uses now is via a feeder road from the **Yaqara** cattle station on the north-west side of Viti Levu to **Nananu** village from where a trail leads over the **Nakauvadra Range** to the head waters of the **Wainibuka River**. Ilai will happily arrange a trip from three to ten days which will also include a boat trip to the island of **Moturiki**. The accommodation, road and sea transportation and food are provided by host families in the villages and the cost per day is F$80 a person.

I've devised a special hike for those who would like to do their own thing. Make sure you are adequately prepared with mosquito nets, insect repellent, flashlight, food such as corned beef, sugar, tea, rice and flour packed to be waterproof; and packets of cigarettes and money in small denominations. If you like fishing, take

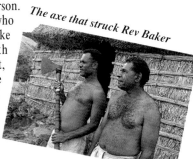

The axe that struck Rev Baker

a casting rod with lures as the rivers are full of bass. A taxi from Nadi up the Sigatoka Valley to Korolevu Village at the end of the road will cost approximately F$100 one way. Stop at Sigatoka to purchase supplies.

If you want to enjoy local flavour and lower cost, 3-tonne trucks, equipped with seats depart Sigatoka for Korolevu between 2pm and 4pm each day except Sunday and cost F$4 per person. Buy a kilogramme of lamb chops and fresh bread for the first night; cheese for sandwiches for lunch the following day and 500g (1.1lb) of *yaqona* for your *sevusevu* (presentation to the chief). Thereafter you can purchase *yaqona* in each village when you first arrive. Divide your purchase into daily rations so you can give your host family two cans of corned beef, a kilogramme of flour, rice, and sugar and a packet of tea and sweets for the children. Double the ration if there are two of you. The men will greatly appreciate a packet of cigarettes.

The car journey will take more than three hours if you stop to

Fishing, Viti Levu

take pictures as you ascend up the valley road. Try and arrive before 2pm so there is plenty of time to make arrangements to spend the night in the village.

On arrival at **Korolevu Village** ask to see the **Turaga ni Koro**. This is the village administrator. Explain that you want to spend the night and then go with him to present your *sevusevu* to the chief. Also explain that you wish to spend a few days up the river on your way to Nubutautau and arrange for someone to go ahead to prepare accommodation at the villages of **Sauvakarua** and **Nubutautau**. Make sure you arrange for a horse to carry baggage and supplies.

Everything is now set for a most enjoyable time. As you leave the next day, present your host family F$15 to F$20 for each guest in your party. Allow F$3 per day for your guide and F$5 for the horse. The guide will be a villager who will be only too happy to take you to the next village. Your host family or the Turaga ni Koro will make the arrangements. Make sure you confirm the fee first. A hard day's trek will take you past the village of **Namoli** to your first destination, **Sauvakarua**.

Next day's march is shorter and brings you to the infamous **Nubutautau,** site of the Rev Baker's misfortune. For those who have time, spend two days in each village. An overnight at the villages of Korolevu, Sauvakarua, Nubutautau, Sauvakarua and return to Korolevu will take four days. Return to Sigatoka on the village truck.

Sauvakarua Village

Savusavu harbour and township

11. Exploring Fiji's North

For those who venture off the beaten track, Fiji's north offers wonderful rewards. Allow at least a week for a general tour, with stays at resorts and islands along the way. There is no fixed itinerary, instead I've given general directions and recommendations on where to stay. Tailor your exploration of this area according to the time you have. Those seeking some of the best scuba diving in the world should plan to make this area their destination for the duration of their holiday.

The 'north' is a general term applied to the islands of Vanua Levu, Taveuni, Qamea, Laucala, Rabi, Kioa, Matagi and the magic islands of the Ringold Isles, Heemskirk Reefs, Qelelevu, Wailangilala and Duff Reef. The largest of these islands is Vanua Levu comprising 5,535sq km (2,137sq miles) and second only to Viti Levu which is nearly double in size. Vanua Levu is irregular in shape, running on a south-west to north-east axis for approximately 161km (100 miles) and seldom exceeding 48km (30 miles) in width.

As in Viti Levu, there is a mountainous interior. This runs the length of the island and is closer to the east coast, where it traps the moisture laden south-east trade winds and so divides the island climatically. The east tends to

Yacht regatta, Savusavu

have much more rain than the west. Sugar cane is grown on the western side and Labasa, which grew up around the sugar mill, rivals Lautoka as Fiji's second largest city.

The easiest way is to fly to **Savusavu** either from Nadi or Suva. Sunflower Airlines flies from Nadi and Fiji Air operates from Suva daily (see *Practical Information*). Savusavu is on the eastern coast of Vanua Levu, at a strategic position about the middle of the island. The township nestles around one of the most beautiful natural harbours in the Pacific and is a port of entry to Fiji.

North Fiji
15 miles / 24 km

Great Sea Reef   Namotu

MACUATA-

NADOGO   Naqumu

Navidamu

YAQAGA

Votua

Nasau   Delanacau
▲ 744 m

Banikea

Bua

Navotuvotu
▲ 842 m   Nadivakarua

YADUA   Sawani   Dawara

Nawaido

Nabouwalu

The commercial centre of Savusavu hugs a narrow coastal strip beside the harbour. **Nawi Island** is immediately offshore and the deep water between the island and the town is a perfect anchorage for visiting yachts. The road follows the bay towards **Lesiaceva Point**. There are a number of hotels and resorts on this stretch. **Na Koro** resort features a reception/dining area in the style of a *bure kalou* (ancient temple) and accommodation *bures* among coconut trees and flowering bougainvillea.

The main road runs north-east over the hill and along the coast, passing **Namale Plantation Resort** and soon after, the **Kon Tiki Resort** which is probably the most interesting in Vanua Levu. The resort was originally built by a local nature-lover who turned the 61ha (150 acres) of the old copra plantation into a perfect hide-

away from the busy world, with walks through its own rainforest where 22 of Fiji's 45 native birds may be observed.

There is a stream with waterfalls and a nine-hole golf course, two tennis courts, volleyball court and for those who cannot unplug completely, a satellite TV link. The resort has a wide frontage to the lagoon and its own small boat harbour with direct access through the bar-

Bure-style Na Roro Resort

rier reef to the sea, offering both excellent scuba diving and deep sea fishing. Accommodation rates begin at F$25 and go up to F$200 per day.

As it was in the past, so too now, the **Hibiscus Highway** between

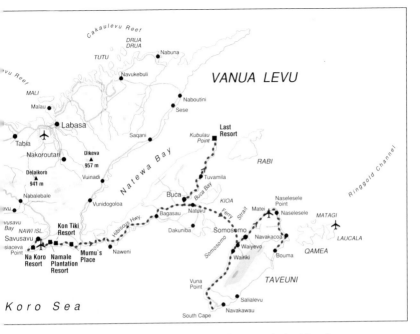

Savusavu and **Buca Bay** attracts interesting people looking for an alternative lifestyle. For some reason, North Americans in particular seem drawn to this part of Fiji. A short distance along the road from the Kon Tiki Resort, a retired US Air Force Colonel, Gordon Edris, has a small place called **Mumu's Place**, open to visitors seeking budget accommodation.

It is 60km (37¼ miles) from Savusavu to Buca Bay along this scenic highway, while another road turns left 3km (1¼ miles) past the Kon Tiki to join **Natewa Bay** and continues for 130km (81 miles) in a grand sweep around the bay, crosses the mountains and eventually reaches **Labasa**, the largest town in Vanua Levu.

The main road continues on past the **Natuvu** turn off (the ferry point to Taveuni) to its terminal at Napuka, passing **Tuvamila** estate owned by Laurie Simpson, son of the famous David Simpson and his wife Dorothy. Laurie, who is 84, still runs the plantation. Accommodation is available in the homestead which has a magnificent, full size billiard table and breathtaking views of Buca Bay and Rabi Island. This is a wonderful place for a few days before continuing to **Taveuni**.

Tuvamila has beautiful bush walks, a mile of black sand beach and offers a chance to experience real plantation life. Call the operator on 84070 and book a call to Tukavesi-Buca Bay, No 17, which will connect with Elle Simpson.

Further along, a syndicate of alternative lifestyle Americans purchased a property at **Kubulau**, just before the end of the road, with the intention of hosting paying visitors and called it

The Simpsons of Tuvamila

The abandoned Last Resort

the **Last Resort**. Sadly, it never achieved its ambition and is now minded by a caretaker.

Two islands offshore, **Rabi** and **Kioa**, are home to different communities. Rabi was purchased for the people of Banaba (Ocean Island) whose home was mined for phosphate. Royalties from the sale of phosphate paid for this magnificent island, while the smaller Kioa Island was purchased on behalf of people from Tuvalu, who earned the purchase price by working for the American Armed Forces during the war against Japan.

A daily bus service from Savusavu departs at 10am and reaches Natuvu in time to connect with a small ferry bound for **Waiyevo** on the island of Taveuni at 1pm. It is a scenic drive with local flavour and to me offers more than a brief plane hop to Taveuni or the ferry trip from Savusavu to Taveuni. If you plan to do just Taveuni and skip Vanua Levu, there is a direct flight from Suva and another one via Savusavu from Nadi.

The ferry from Natuvu often stops at Kioa on its way to Taveuni and then continues to the settlement of Waiyevo at about the middle of the island on the north-west coast. Taveuni is Fiji's third largest island and geologically, its most recent. It is of volcanic origin and is known as the 'garden isle' because of its rich soils and luxuriant vegetation which includes large tracts of rainforest and a profusion of bird life.

The 180th meridian of longitude passes through Taveuni island at a point slightly to the west of Waiyevo and in theory it is possible to straddle this line where it passes through the road so that one foot will be in 'today' and the other in 'yesterday'. However, for purposes of keeping Fiji in the same time zone, this distinction is often ignored.

A copra plantation

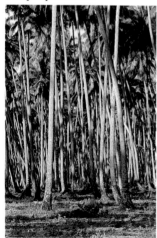

Soon after crossing the dateline, you reach the settlement of **Wairiki**, dominated by a large Catholic Church and a cross on a hill above it. The spot marks the scene of a crucial battle where the hitherto undefeated forces of the Tongan Ma'afu suffered a decisive loss from the locals led by the Tui Cakau.

The fertility and climate of Taveuni attracted European planters and some of the estates are owned by their descendants to this day. The Soqulu estate, 3km (1¼ miles) south of Wairiki, was part of an ambitious subdivision in the 1970s by an American. The large copra plantation was turned into a community with a club house, tennis courts, a small but fascinating golf course and a series of tar-sealed roads from the sea shore up the mist shrouded mountains.

Spear dance, Somosomo Village

Blocks of land were sold and a number of people built houses, some among rainforest on the hillside overlooking Somosomo Strait between Taveuni and Vanua Levu. Despite the magnificent views the development never realised its full potential.

It is 20km (12½ miles) from Waiyevo to **Vuna** at the southern end and an additional 7km (4¼ miles) to **South Cape**. The drive north-east from Waiyevo is equally spectacular. The road passes the settlement and village of **Somosomo**, seat of the Tui Cakau (Lord of the Reef), paramount chief of the province of Cakaudrove. The current incumbent, Ratu Sir Penaia Ganilau, is also the President of Fiji. It continues along the coast to **Naselesele Point** and the airport at **Matei** and then bears to the south-east to reveal a colourful lagoon dotted with small islands and the bigger islands of **Qamea** and **Laucala**. There are a number of places offering accommodation near the airport.

Navakacoa landing, 8km (5 miles) from the airport, is the pick up point for the islands of Qamea, Laucala and **Matagi**. Each island has a resort hotel. Laucala was purchased by publishing tycoon, the late Malcolm Forbes, who turned it into a private playground and willed his remains to be interred on the island. The island has a small, exclusive resort with an all-inclusive rate of F$500 per person per day.

Probably the most attractive resort in the north of Fiji is at

Matagi Island with Horse Shoe Bay

Matagi Island, a 97-ha (240-acre) copra plantation operated by the Douglas family. The island lies 10km (6¼ miles) from **Navakacoa** landing, and the resort with its distinct *bures*, built on a hexagonal plan is sited beside a beautiful white sand beach facing **Qamea Island** with a blue lagoon between. The family-run resort is limited to 24 guests at any one time and operates two live-aboard dive vessels, taking full advantage of some of the most superb diving and cruising in the world. The opposite side of the island has the famous **Horse Shoe Bay** and beach. There is a full programme of activities, including village tours and an excursion to the **Bouma** falls on Taveuni. The rate begins at F$115 per day.

It is 7km (4¼ miles) from Navakacoa landing to the Bouma waterfalls. There is a nominal admission fee and a five-minute walk to the waterfalls which is one of the most spectacular in Fiji. A large volume of water gushes more than 22m (70ft) to a pool surrounded by rainforest. A swim and picnic (barbecue facilities available on site) are highly recommended.

12. Toberua Island Resort

A number of small and super exclusive resorts in Fiji, some with private beaches to frolic on and prices to match, guarantee a sinfully self-indulgent experience.

Fiji's 300 islands offer something for everyone, and resorts have been built to cater for every taste and budget from multi millionaires to backpackers. **Toberua Island**, tucked away among a maze of coral reefs in Fiji's Bau Waters between the mainland of Viti Levu and the island of Ovalau, and several others such as **Wakaya**, **Vatulele**, **Turtle Island** and **Kaimbu** resorts are in a category and class apart.

Each of these island resorts limits the number of guests to a small number and then pampers and spoils them. Some like Kaimbu Island in northern Lau are so exclusive that there are only three luxurious guest cottages, each with its own beach, and a rate of US$995 per couple per day.

Toberua Island Resort is a gem. This tiny island of 1.6ha

Reef golf at Toberua at low tide

(4 acres) is a miniature botanic garden with 14 guest *bures* built by Fijian craftsmen in a style that honours their highest chiefs.

Toberua Island Resort was one of the first in Fiji to see the need for a small exclusive island resort and set about creating the conditions and ambience which would appeal to the discerning traveller. Toberua does not only provide luxurious accommodation and supe-

A beach to call your own

rior cuisine – many places in the world can do this – but has succeeded in creating an atmosphere where the unique nature of the island, the Fijian staff and the culture of the people in nearby villages has melded into harmonious style. Guests begin their adventure from the **Nakelo** landing beside an old trading post on the **Navualoa River,** in the heart of the Rewa River delta which lies a few minutes from the Nausori International Airport. The 40-minute boat ride down the river is a most appropriate way to begin the holiday.

The island is within sight of some of Fiji's most historic landmarks. To the north-west is the island of **Bau**, the seat of Fiji's highest chiefs; to the south-west the **Kaba Peninsula** where Fiji's last great battle was fought; to the north-east, the island of **Ovalau** and the old capital, **Levuka**.

The daily programme includes many options – even playing golf on the reef at low tide! Besides the usual assortment of seasports like paddle boards, hobie cats and windsurfers, there are fishing trips and scuba diving for certified divers, and of course, snorkelling. For nature lovers, there are boat trips to nearby villages and to uninhabited sand keys and bird sanctuary islands as well as picnics at these romantic locations.

Toberua Island Resort can be reached directly at Tel: 479177, Fax: 302215 or at the Suva office, Tel: 302356. There is a price to pay for exclusivity, though. Reckon on spending at least F$550 per couple a day on accommodation, food and beverages, and transfers to and from the island.

Toberua Island lies among a maze of reefs in the Bau Waters

Activities

13. Scuba Diving

For many years it was a well-kept secret that Fiji had something special to offer the dedicated scuba diver. The secret is out now and even though there are more than 30 operators who offer diving services, including certification training, there are so many islands and the reef complex is so vast, that only a minuscule part of it is regularly seen by visiting divers.

One of many dive sites in Fiji

This may change one day, but never to the point that dive locations become too crowded. One of the most attractive aspects of scuba diving in Fiji is the great variety it offers.

The names of some of the famous dive sites suggest their diversity: The Blue Ribbon Eel Reef, The Ledge, Fish Factory Corner, Cabbage Patch, Korolevu, Jack's Place, Yellow Tunnel, Barracuda Hole, Small White Wall, Annie's Bommie, The Zoo. The bonus is that all these sites are within one location!

There are amazing underwater experiences to be had. Take as an example, The Great White Wall of Taveuni. The dive commences by entering a tunnel at the top of the reef at a depth of 9m (30ft) and exiting at 27½m (90ft) on the face of a vertical wall covered with a lush, profuse growth of soft white coral as far as the eye can see.

Patrolling the face of the wall is an abundance of multi-coloured fish, so tame that they brush fearlessly against you. Next, you ascend to 17m (55ft) and enter another tunnel which takes you to the top of the reef at 11m (35ft).

As Bill Gleason writes in Skin Diver Magazine: "When every island claims to be the ultimate travel adventure, the extraordinary disappears and what is described as the 'ultimate' becomes common. Welcome to the islands of Fiji where the extraordinary still exists. For here the knowledgeable and discriminating diver can find superb world class diving, a different and friendly culture and a variety of accommodations...

"Unlike the Caribbean, where Cozumel is Cozumel and Bonaire is Bonaire, there is no single Fiji... there are many different areas to dive and it is impossible to see all of them even on a two-week trip."

It is significant that for three years in a row – 1990, 1991 and 1992 – the Cousteau Society has chosen Fiji as the 'Pacific Ocean Search' expedition venue for its members. This is a wonderful testimonial not only to the superb diving, but also to Fiji as a destination.

There are now a number of small resorts catering almost exclusively for divers. These are invariably located near the best dive sites. Some of these sites are **Beqa Island**, **Kadavu Island** and **Astrolabe Lagoon**, **Wakaya Island**, **Savusavu Barrier Reef**, **Namenalala Island**, and **Taveuni**, **Matagi**, **Qamea** and **Laucala** islands.

What can you expect to find? A profusion of tropical corals and fish life in a bewildering kaleidoscope. Caves, overhangs, walls and drop offs with soft and hard corals, gorgonians, fan corals and large fish, including sharks.

An itinerary can be arranged to offer a number of different locations or a booking can be made on a live-aboard dive boat. Rather than recommend any particular diving spot or boat, I suggest that the serious diver with no knowledge of Fiji should get in touch with **Sea Fiji Limited** at 850345 or Fax: 850344 for a special itinerary which will be developed based on a questionnaire sent by the company. They will arrange everything, including air transportation.

Diving in Fiji has something for everyone – the novice and the professional, so that when you leave, it is with the feeling that you've experienced something unique.

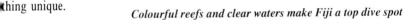

Colourful reefs and clear waters make Fiji a top dive spot

14. Fishing

Fishing in Fiji can be divided into a number of different categories. There is deep sea game fishing which includes such renowned fish as

marlin, sailfish, yellowfin, dogtooth tuna, shark, wahoo, giant trevally and mahimahi (dolphin fish).

There is fishing for ground fish which the whole family can enjoy in the shelter of the lagoon, and there is fishing from the shore, where the true angler casts his lure among patches of coral to hook the powerful tropical trevallys, bar-

Lobsters for the picking

racuda, queenfish, coral trout and Spanish mackerel.

Finally, there is the art of fly fishing for the wily bonefish on tidal flats. The rivers have largemouth bass and it is possible to either drive to remote and beautiful places for a day's fishing, or to arrange a punt or an inflatable raft to drift downstream while casting for fish.

Most of the resort hotels include game fishing as part of the optional activities available to guests. Some of the resorts own and operate their own boats; others operate in association with subcontracting companies. One resort, the **Ocean Pacific Club**, near Suva, specialises in catering to game fishing enthusiasts.

How good is fishing in Fiji? As good as, if not better than in Hawaii, says Max Lane, whose resort is the only one in Fiji that specialises in looking after fishermen. Lane also runs the only liveaboard fishing boat and on a recent five-day trip on the *Adi Kuila,* caught and released one marlin and had five others strike the lure.

Unlike Hawaii or New Zealand where there are scores of game fishing boats, Fiji's waters are relatively unexploited. Most of the areas where grand billfish would be expected to run are seldom fished at all.

Prices for a day's deep sea game fishing in Fiji will depend on the type of boat but can cost more than F$1,000. Smaller boats will cost F$500 and up. The *Adi Kuila*, which accommodates six people, costs F$1,200 per day including all meals and tackle, and F$860 for a full day's charter.

Those who would like to know how to get the best out of fishing in Fiji should contact Max Lane at 303252 or on fax 361577.

Right: grinning with their catch

Shopping

Shopping in Fiji falls into several categories. There is a local market which tends to divide between the indigenous Fijians and Indian migrants who form a large part of the population. Much of the difference between the two races and their culture is reflected in what is purchased in personal items, food and jewellery. There is also a thriving market place for visitors which offers duty free electronics, watches, cameras, perfumes, gems, gold and brand name products from Europe and Asia. Fijian handicrafts and artifacts are the final category and range from well executed traditional items to carvings and gift items for the tourist trade. There is something for everyone.

Jewellery

As a general rule, prices for jewellery are cheaper in Fiji than it is in Europe, Australia, New Zealand, USA and even Singapore and Hong Kong. Much depends on the person shopping as it is often possible to bargain. The feeling of having got a bargain can be most satisfying although how much of a bargain, only an expert

One of the many duty free shops that line Suva town

Gold jewellery is a bargain

who knows real values would be able to tell.

As a general guide, a wedding band of 22K gold, for example costs approximately F$50 in Fiji whereas the same ring would cost more than double the price in Europe. One reason for lower prices is that gold in Fiji is sold by weight whereas small items in other countries are sold by the piece. Precious stones are also cheaper. A 2K emerald ring in Fiji sells for approximately F$10,000; a 1K, D grade, G colour diamond for F$14,000 whereas its price in, say, Australia would be more than F$20,000.

Lower prices are made possible in Fiji because, in part, merchants have to consider the local market which is neither large or wealthy. Overheads, determined by rents and labour costs, are also lower in Fiji and the Indian shopkeepers who control most of the industry are prepared to accept a smaller return. Armed with this knowledge, the happy shopper can walk the streets of Nadi, Suva, Lautoka or Sigatoka looking for bargains.

Handicrafts

Jacks Handicrafts Limited at the Sheraton Resort (Tel: 700083), Main Street, Nadi town (Tel: 700744) and Sigatoka (Tel: 500810) is excellent for a wide range of products. Novelty items, handicrafts and artifacts, books, clothes, jewellery and even an extensive collection of Pacific Islands sea shells, including expensive collectors items such as the golden cowrie, are available at good prices.

There is no doubt that you get what you pay for and the choice is formidable. Handicrafts and artifacts include well-made replicas of old weapons, bowls used for ritual purposes, *yaqona* bowls, baskets, *masi* cloth and fans. It is illegal to take out *tabua* (sperm whale teeth) which are of great ritual value in Fiji.

It is possible to find antiques. One 500-year-old clay pot has just been found, but

Curio shops and woodcrafts

rarely are these in mint condition as most items were made from wood and are therefore prone to the ravages of time. The National Museum has a fine collection and so do some of the old European families, but the Museum certainly won't part with theirs and it is unlikely a visitor will find families who will sell in the short time they are in the country. Asking around at villages may produce stone adzes. These are bound to be genuine as it takes so much effort to make one, no one would want to duplicate it as there is no demand.

Electronic Goods

There are scores of duty free shops with cameras, electronic equipment, watches and perfume. **Cumming Street** in **Suva** is crowded with duty free shops. For top quality hi-fidelity equipment try **Maneklal's** 141 Vitogo Parade, **Lautoka**, Tel: 665242. Maneklal and his two sons import the best brand names and offer a selection of top of the line equipment at good prices. These are generally between 10 and 20 percent lower than most other countries, depending on the item.

Clothing

There are also dozens of clothes stores with an excellent selection of tee-shirts and casual wear. Fiji is a major exporter of clothing to Australia, New Zealand and the United States. Prices are low in comparison, even for some of the better

Cotton sulus

clothes. There is a very good selection of hand-dyed muslin cotton *sulus*. This is the Fijian name for the wraparound known throughout the Pacific as *sarong*, *lava lava* and *pareo*. Prices range from F$10 to F$15 for muslin cotton *sulus* and much less for other types of material. Wearing a *sulu* is fun and most practical as well.

Municipal Markets

Each town has a municipal market which opens early in the morning and closes at 5pm. They are always colourful. Friday and Saturday mornings is the busiest with vendors spilling onto the footpaths and even onto the road. Fresh vegetables, root crops, seasonal fruit such as avocado, pineapple, mango, papaya and banana, spices essential for Indian cuisine, piles of dried *yaqona* and local tobacco cured into coils are usually on display.

Municipal market, Suva

Yaqona (piper mysthisticum) roots are pounded into powder and mixed with water to produce a mildly narcotic drink to which most of the population, both Fijian and Indian, are extremely partial to. *Yaqona* has an impor-

Cassava for sale

tant ritual significance in Fijian culture. An elaborate ceremony surrounds its presentation, preparation and serving. Visitors will have many opportunities to taste it. A slight numbing of the mouth is the immediate effect. It takes a great deal of *yaqona* (imbibing over several hours) to produce a mildly euphoric state. Regular drinkers experience a quicker response.

Municipal markets offer the best opportunity for absorbing the local scene. Suva has the largest (see Itinerary 1, *Pick & Mix* section). You can stand to one side with a slice of fresh pineapple or melon in hand and watch the press of people without a sense of intrusion.

Shopping Tips

A word of caution. It can be fun strolling down the streets of Nadi, Lautoka, Suva or Sigatoka. The air is usually heavy with the smell of incense, loud Hindi music and the aroma of spicy foods. Sometimes the Indian shopkeepers can be over enthusiastic with their 'g'day mate!' They try to get customers into their store any way they can. Most visitors take it in their stride. Some find it annoying.

Beware of Fijians who seem eager to make friends, especially the so-called 'sword sellers'. Genuine friendliness of the Fijian people is so disarming that most visitors to Suva, Nadi and Lautoka fall easy prey to these rascals who trade on it. They first make friends with a cheery 'bula!' or 'hello, mate!'.

They inquire about your family, country of origin and finally ask your name while at the same time fishing out a piece of wood in the shape of a sword and carving your name on it, and then demanding

Shell and handicraft market

an exorbitant sum for this piece of junk. There are only about a dozen sword sellers and if you should happen to strike one and he starts carving your name, just walk away. Just keep walking no matter what he may say. Do not look back. If necessary, walk into the nearest store and ask the shopkeeper to call the police. There is nothing he can do and you will save yourself a great deal of anger and the chance of a ruined holiday. Beware also of 'guides' who promise to take you to shops where you will get the 'best' bargains.

Eating Out

Fiji's multi-racial mix reflects well in its cuisine. Here you will find European food (with a French bias) prepared by leading chefs in the major resorts; Chinese (predominantly Cantonese but with some styles from other parts of China); Indian with its emphasis on chillies and spices; ethnic Fijian; and a blending of styles so that a smorgasbord presentation may include some of each.

Fijian Cuisine

As a guest at the Captain's table, on his way to England, the late Ratu Sir Edward Cakobau was clearly not amused when questioned about Fiji's cannibal past. He solemnly studied the menu for some time, turned to the waiter and without batting an eyelid replied: "The menu does not appear very interesting. Could you please bring me the passenger list?"

Man-eating jokes aside, Fijian cuisine relies on fresh food, cooked simply, usually by boiling. Coconut cream, pressed from the flesh of the nut, is either added during the cooking or served as a sauce. When it is added during the cooking it is called *lolo*, and *miti* when used as a sauce.

Sunday is always a feast day as in biblical times. Fijians are

Sunday lunch after church

Christians and punctilious about observing the Sabbath. This day is reserved for worship and family get-togethers around a noon feast immediately after service. Economic circumstances determine the food that is served, but even in villages where there is limited cash income, the number of dishes will nevertheless be impressive: fresh fish, shellfish, seaweed and *beche de mer* from the lagoon, various root crops and vegetables, chicken and sometimes meat, and cakes and puddings made from bananas and papaya and fresh fruit. Often

there will also be a Fijian version of chop suey and curry. Favourites such as *kokoda* (fresh, cubed fish marinated in lemon juice and coconut cream) are served with hot chilli peppers.

The *lovo* is a Pacific Islands speciality. It is an ingenious way of cooking food. A pit is dug and lined with river stones. A fire is set on the stones, with more stones

Placing food in a **lovo**

placed on the pieces of wood. The size of the pit and of the stones depend on the amount of food to be cooked. It may be the size of a small swimming pool where a mountain of food will be cooked including whole pigs, turtles, fish, beef, root crops and vegetables. In former times it was also the principal means of cooking human flesh.

The fire is allowed to die down and the unburnt pieces and embers are removed and the stones levelled. Green mid-ribs of coconut fronds are placed over the hot stones and food wrapped in leaves but more

often in foil, is placed on the sticks so that it will not come in direct contact with the stones. Banana leaves and sacking cover the pit. Soil is then heaped over the *lovo* to trap the heat inside. Two hours later, the 'oven' is opened and the food is ready to be served. Most hotels and resorts feature *lovo* nights, usually accompanied by Fijian entertainment.

Recommendations

Apart from restaurants recommended in the itineraries, the following are some of my personal favourites. Arguably, the best food is served at the best hotels. The **Sheraton** and **Regent** resorts at Denarau Island, Nadi, each have a number of

Live crabs ready for the pot

restaurants which serve Fijian, Indian, Chinese and European dishes as well as buffets and *lovos*. Prices depend on the restaurant but can be up to F\$50 for a main course, though it is possible to have an evening meal for less than F\$20 not including drinks. Average price per person for a three-course dinner without drinks is categorized as follows: Expensive = F\$30 and above, Moderate = F\$21–F\$29, Inexpensive = F\$20 and below.

Nadi

THE SHERATON RESORT
Denarau Island
Tel: 701777
Four restaurants to choose from:
PORTS OF CALL
Dinner only. Expensive.
MALOLO RESTAURANT
Dinner only. Expensive.
VERANDAH
An extensive buffet breakfast, lunch and dinner. Moderate.
OCEAN LANAI
Lunch and dinner. Inexpensive.
THE CAFE
Light meals from 10am–10pm. Good food, well presented in very pleasant surroundings. Inexpensive.

THE REGENT RESORT
Denarau Island
Tel: 780000
GARDEN VIEW
Dinner only. Expensive.
STEAK HOUSE
Lunch and dinner. Superb salad bar. Moderate to Expensive.
OCEAN TERRACE
Breakfast and dinner. Expensive.
Swiss chef commands a battery of local and expatriate chefs for a varied menu and good food.

COFFEE LOUNGE
360 Main Street
Tel: 701122
Very clean restaurant serving good and cheap Indian vegetarian food. A combination *thali* (platter) includes *roti* (unleavened bread), *dhal, papadam, samosas*, curry and rice. Cheaper dishes available as well as various combinations and home-made ice cream in many flavours. There is an espresso machine. Open daily for lunch except Sunday. Inexpensive.

CURRY HOUSE
11 Sagayam Road
Tel: 700960
Once The Curry Corner, Curry House serves a full range of curries including crab and lobster when available at prices which begin at F$4.50. Open daily, including Sunday, from 9am–10pm. Inexpensive.

HAMACHO JAPANESE RESTAURANT
Martintar
Tel: 790252
Genuine Japanese cuisine prepared by two Japanese chefs. Try the set course dinner. Open 5.30–10pm daily, including Sunday. Moderate.

CHOPSTICKS AND SEAFOOD RESTAURANT
Main Street
Tel: 700178
Good Cantonese food, F$5–F$8. 9am–10pm daily including Sunday. Inexpensive.

POONS RESTAURANT
Main Street
Tel: 700896
Superlative Cantonese cuisine. Open 10am–10pm daily, including Sunday. Inexpensive.

CARDO'S
Main Street
Tel: 780704
Popular steak house and meeting place for locals who patronise the bar for after-work drinks. Cardo also runs the Roaring Thunder Whitewater Rafting on the Ba River. Open 6–11pm daily. Inexpensive.

Lautoka

CITY TAKEAWAYS
15 Malau Place
Tel: 660001
Cheap but excellent curries and takeaways. Some of the best curries in Fiji. Also serves Chinese dishes. Open from 6am–8pm daily, except Sunday. Inexpensive.

GREAT WALL OF CHINA
21 Naviti Street
Tel: 664775
Good Chinese food and an interesting menu which includes *beche de mer* for those who would like to try it. Chinese people believe in its potency and science suggests there is a good basis for their belief as the flesh has more than 40 percent protein by volume and more than 21 percent minerals. Open daily from 8am–10pm including Sunday. Inexpensive.

Suva

RED LION RESTAURANT
215 Victoria Parade
Tel: 312968
Steak and seafood. Meal also earns admission to Lucky Eddie's and Rockefeller's nightclubs (see *Nightlife*) – all part of the Red Lion complex developed by Liam Hindle and his wife. Hindle is a retired geologist who enjoys good food and wine with a passion. A good deal of humour, or nostalgia as the decor of the Red Lion is reminiscent of Tudor England. Being a major importer and distributor of wine through the Victoria Wine Company gives Hindle the opportunity to visit some of the top vineyards and wineries around the world and he claims he has the best selection available in Fiji. As many of the top resorts and hotels are his clients, there is a good chance he is right. Opens for dinner daily except Sunday and for lunch on Friday. Moderate.

O'REILLEY'S BRASSERIE
5 McArthur Street
Tel: 312884
Opens daily for lunch and throughout the evening. Sometimes includes entertainment. Offers good food and the opportunity of meeting interesting local people in a most pleasant and convivial atmosphere.
Inexpensive.

PIZZA HUT
207 Victoria Parade
Tel: 311825
Open daily for lunch and dinner, pizza and pasta except Sunday, when it is open only for dinner from 7pm. Inexpensive.

THE OLD MILL COTTAGE
49 Carnarvon Street
Tel: 312134
Tucked away from the city centre towards Government buildings, but worth the walk. Only restaurant in Suva serving Fijian, Indian, European and Chinese dishes. Lunch attracts expatriates, Fijian civil servants, lawyers from the nearby law courts and visitors. The food is good with a lunchtime selection which allows any number of combinations: Indian, Fijian and Chinese on the same plate, if you so wish! Open daily for breakfast and lunch except Sunday.
Inexpensive.

CASTLE RESTAURANT
6 Fenton Street, Lami
Tel: 361223
Good Cantonese food in pleasant surroundings. Open daily for lunch and dinner except Sunday. Inexpensive.

LANTERN PALACE
10 Pratt Street
Tel: 314633
Cantonese food of great consistency makes this one of the most popular restaurants. Lunch and dinner daily except Sunday. Inexpensive.

THE GREAT WOK
Corner Bau Street & Laucala Bay Road
Tel: 301285
Sichuan food, well prepared and served in most pleasant atmosphere. Lunch and dinner daily except Sunday. Inexpensive.

HARE KRISHNA VEGETARIAN RESTAURANTS
16 Pratt Street
Tel: 314154
37 Cumming Street
Tel: 312259
Excellent vegetarian food served in any combination chosen by customer. Open daily for lunch except Sunday. Inexpensive.

TIKOS FLOATING RESTAURANT AND BAR
Stinson Parade
Tel: 313626
Steak and seafood in a former cruise boat moored off Stinson Parade in the heart of the city and popular with locals. Open daily for lunch and dinner except Sunday. Moderate.

SUVA TRAVELODGE
Victoria Parade
Tel: 301600
LALI RESTAURANT
Lunch and dinner daily, except weekends. Sunday poolside barbecue. Moderate.
PENNYS RESTAURANT
Daily from 6am–11pm for breakfast, lunch and evening meals. Moderate.

Nightlife

The kind of nightlife you look for in Fiji will depend on how dangerously you wish to live. A drunk is a drunk is a drunk and can be either a nuisance or a menace. Fiji is a small place and the choice of places to go to at night are limited. There is no national orchestra, no ballet and no theatre. Hotels have resident bands and discos. In those places, you are likely to see other tourists and seldom locals.

On the other hand, nightclubs which cater mainly for locals can sometimes become volatile as excitement, fanned by loud music, drink and the presence of pretty girls has unpredictable effects on village boys and can result in either a fist fight or a riot.

Most nightclubs in Fiji will continue until the early hours or as long as there is a large crowd present; the exception being Saturday when it is supposed to stop at the stroke of midnight because of the Sunday Observance Decree.

Locally-brewed beer

Nadi

In the Nadi area, the **Planters Club** at the Sheraton Resort, Denarau Island, Tel: 701777, stands out. You are likely to find quite a few of the local people enjoying the ambience. The atmosphere is lively and exciting and the security is tight. The barmen are competent and dance behind the bar while serving their customers. The best nights are Fridays and Saturdays when the locals arrive in large numbers.

When the action proves too hot it is nice to step out and cool off on the edge of one of the pools in the foyer or stroll to the swimming pool near the beach. The **Malolo Lounge**, next to the Planters Club, features a resident band and a more languid pace.

For those who want more of the local scene, **Ed's Bar**, Tel: 790373, and **Jessica's Nightclub**, Tel: 790044, at Martintar be-

Hotels often feature entertainment from Polynesia

tween the Nadi International Airport and Nadi town, are the places to go. Weekends are always the busiest. Ed's Bar tends to attract a more cosmopolitan crowd whereas Jessica's is the haunt of the younger set. Friday is the busiest and the action continues till the early hours of the morning.

Saturday hours are restricted to midnight in deference to the Sunday Observance Decree, but often no one pays attention to this and the partying seems to continue past the hour.

Suva

Because it is the largest metropolitan centre in Fiji, Suva also has the most varied nightlife. As in the west, this is almost entirely confined to bars and nightclubs. The major hotels, **Travelodge**, **Courtesy Inn** and **Tradewinds Hotel** are the best for casual drinks during the day.

O'Reillys Brasserie is a notch above most other establishments and also serves lunch at reasonable prices. It attracts an interesting crowd of locals and expatriates. It is part of a complex established by a former geologist and his wife, which includes the **Pizza Hut**, **Queensland Arcade** snack bar (complete with an espresso machine), **Red Lion** restaurant and **Lucky Eddie's** and **Rockefeller's** nightclubs, Tel: 312884. All are popular with locals and visitors alike and have the advantage of being next to each other on **Victoria Parade**, Suva's main Street.

The nightclubs charge a nominal admission fee and drinks are inexpensive by world standards. Friday nights tend to be jam-packed, but Lucky Eddie's is busy from midweek; the patrons represent a broad cross-section of Fiji's multi-racial society. You will find Fijians, Indians, Europeans, other Pacific Islanders and every possible combination in between, all having a good time.

Some of the most attractive people in the world will be gyrating to loud music. Visitors can play the interesting game of trying to establish the less obvious ethnic combinations. Fiji seems to have them all. There are part-Europeans, part-Chinese, part-Rotumans, part-Indians and sometimes part-everything!

Dinner at the Red Lion restaurant earns free admission to Rockefeller's and Lucky Eddie's. This represents a small saving for a large party as admission is F$4 per person Thursday through Saturday, and F$2 on other nights. Suva is not a large city and it's likely you will see the same faces at different spots during the night.

Two other popular watering places are nearby: **Traps**, Tel: 312922, and the **Golden Dragon**, Tel: 311018, just along the way on Victoria Parade, probably the oldest surviving nightclub in Suva. Traps has a similar clientele to O'Reilly's, Rockefeller's and Lucky Eddie's and the crowd tends to flow from one joint to another during the course of the night.

By 11pm everyone is in place for the duration of the evening. The Golden Dragon attracts its own band of followers but it tends to be less cosmopolitan, unless you count the Taiwanese, Korean and Japanese fishermen whose boats happen to be in port for an overhaul. My recommendation would be to have a late dinner at the Pizza Hut or the Red Lion and then check out Lucky Eddie's or Rockefeller's, or both, for a most pleasant evening.

Nightlife on resorts is low-key

There are other places but I would not go there if you paid me. Some visitors to Fiji, however, may crave a great deal more adventure and taxi drivers will be only too happy to make suggestions. Good luck!

Nightlife away from the main centres and on the smaller islands is usually restricted to the principal resorts although even small ones have a string band and a dance floor. The bigger hotels have bands with amplified instruments and some have discos as well. The action depends on the crowd.

Calendar of Special Events

Fiji lacks the ancient festivals and carnivals of other parts of the world, except for those introduced by its migrants who celebrate Easter, Christmas, the Hindu festival of Diwali (Festival of Lights) and the Muslim fasting month of Ramadan. Events which may have been celebrated by Fijians before the introduction of Christianity are now no more except for some exceptions. These ceremonies, which are observed at the deaths of prominent chiefs and the installation of their successors, survive in modified form and are spectacular to observe. Hotel tour desk staff usually know of such events.

Hindus perform fire walking as an act of faith. Such events are not scheduled, the date being determined by a temple priest. Once the date is set, the event is usually publicised to attract the public; the admission fee charged is used for charitable purposes. These are probably the most spectacular events as devotees, after a two-week period of preparation which involves abstinence from sexual intercourse and a restricted diet, assemble in the temple, march to the nearest river or the sea for ritual cleansing. They then skewer their faces and bodies with silver pins and in a trance, finally arrive at the temple to walk

Hindu fire-walking ceremony

over a bed of coals.

Festivals such as the Hibiscus Festival in Suva in August, the Sugar Festival in Lautoka in September and the Bula Festival in Nadi in July are of recent origin and no doubt will eventually become part of the fabric of the country in the near future. As dates vary from year to year, check with the Fiji Visitors Bureau (Suva, Tel: 302433 or Nadi, Tel: 722433) for precise dates of the festivals. The Visitors Bureau usually has a list of coming events.

July

Bula Festival. A week-long festival with daily entertainment, culminating in a procession of floats, brass bands, marching girls and beauty queens through the streets of Nadi.

Festival grounds have an amusement park with carnival rides.

August

Hibiscus Festival. Fiji's biggest festival. Originally begun as something for the tourists, it is now a week of fun for the locals. The festival features a programme of nightly entertainment and culminates in a procession of floats through the streets of Suva and a grand finale at Albert Park on Saturday night when the new queen, acknowledged as Fiji's loveliest, is chosen.

September

Sugar City Festival. A week of fun in Lautoka in much the same vein as the Hibiscus Festival in Suva.

October/November

Diwali. A Hindu festival of lights in honour of the goddess Laxmi. Thousands of clay lamps are lit by Hindu devotees around homes throughout the country, people visit each other and exchange gifts of sweets. Some of the wealthy merchants also festoon their homes with displays of flashing electric lights.

November/December

Ratu Bilibili Festival (chief bamboo raft festival). This is without doubt

Ratu Bilibili Festival

Fiji's most striking festival when more than 30 large bamboo rafts, complete with houses and cooking places, known as *bilibili* sail down the Wainimala River to its confluence with the Rewa River and then onto Nausori town where they camp to raise money for their district.

The fleet arrives, holds a fund-raising carnival in town and then the people depart, having disposed of their rafts to willing buyers who want the bamboo used in the construction of the rafts. The people also bring produce which is sold as part of the fund raising. During former times when there were no roads or powered craft, much of the produce from the fertile Rewa, Wainibuka and Wainimala River valleys made its way to Nausori on the bamboo *bilibili*.

Public Holidays

In addition to the variable dates for Easter and Good Friday (April), Diwali (October/November) and Prophet Mohammed's Birthday, the following are public holidays:

New Year's Day	January 1
Ratu Sukuna Day	May 31
Queen's Birthday	June 14
Constitution Day	July 26th
Fiji Day	October 11
Prince Charles Birthday	November 15
Christmas Day	December 25
Boxing Day	November 26

Practical Information

GETTING THERE

Australia is three and a half hours away by plane. There are direct flights to Fiji from Australia, New Zealand, Japan, mainland United States through Honolulu and from Tahiti through Rarotonga. Principal international carriers are Air New Zealand, Qantas, Air Caledonia International and Air Nauru. Fiji's national airline, Air Pacific, maintains scheduled flights to Australia, New Zealand, Japan and to the nearby islands of Tonga and Vanuatu. Air New Zealand has flights from London and Frankfurt which deliver passengers to Fiji. Qantas offers a similar service from Europe and the United States. Be sure to check with your travel agent for the various pack-

ages on offer. There are no direct ship passenger services although cruise boats from Australia often include Fiji in their itineraries. Strict laws govern the entry of yachts in Fiji. Yachtsmen must first clear Health, Immigration and Customs formalities at a designated port of entry. Permission in writing is required if they intend to visit other islands. Immigration officials will advise.

Arriving

Nadi International Airport is the main gateway and has the usual modern facilities. A second airport at Nausori, near Suva, also caters for some international flights with smaller aircraft such as the Boeing 737s operated by Air Pacific and Air Nauru. Buses, rental car offices and taxis are located at the airports (see *Getting About*). When leaving Fiji, visitors are required to pay F$10 departure tax at the check-in counter.

TRAVEL ESSENTIALS

When to Visit

There is no real 'season' for visiting Fiji. Australians and New Zealanders tend to favour the months of June, July, August, September and October during the course of the Southern Hemisphere winter. Visitors from the Northern Hemisphere will find Fiji most attractive November through May when their own countries may be cold and thoughts of beautiful white-sand beaches and warm tropical south sea lagoons are attractive.

Climate and Clothing

Fiji enjoys a tropical maritime climate. Maximum summer temperatures (November–April) average 30°C (86°F). The winter maximum average (May–October) is 26°C (79°F). It gets much cooler in the uplands of the interior of the large islands. Fiji's 'summer' and 'winter' occur in direct contrast to the Northern Hemisphere so that when it is snowing in New York, it is sunny and hot in Fiji. There is, of course, no real winter. A cooling tradewind blows from the east-south-east for most of the year. It usually drops to a whisper in the evening and picks up again by mid-morning.

The mountainous nature of the principal islands has a direct effect on climate. The prevailing east-south-east trade winds meet the mountainous barrier and deposits rain. This is great for vegetation but not so good for tourists. For this reason, most of the hotels and resorts in Fiji are located on the western or 'dry' side of the island of Viti Levu, mostly within close proximity to Nadi international airport.

December to April is also the time when tropical cyclones, formed to the north-west of Fiji, begin trekking south and sometimes pass over the group. The cyclones usually bring winds with gusts of up to and over 100 knots near their centre and heavy rain. There is ample warning from the meteorological office and the hotels and resorts are experienced in coping with problems associated with cyclones. Bad weather usually lasts no more than 24 hours. Cyclones do not necessarily occur each year. There was a period from 1967 to 1980 when Fiji recorded only one.

Having escaped the wrath of destructive cyclones for 20 years, Fiji was visited by two cyclones in quick succession – the relatively mild cyclone Joni in December at the close of 1992 and the more disastrous cyclone Kina which arrived on the second day of 1993. The resulting floods were the worst in more than 100 years. Tourist infrastructure, built to withstand the winds were not affected, although villages and farmers in the river valley networks received the brunt of the rains.

Visitors to Fiji need a light tropical wardrobe. Bathing suits, shorts, tee-shirts and as they will soon discover, *sulus* (known also throughout the Pacific as *pareo* or *sarong*), are a must for both men and women. There are at least 10 different ways in which women can use it, even for evening wear. The largest Christian denomination in Fiji is Wesleyan (Methodist) and visitors are asked to be careful not to offend local sensibilities. Wearing bikinis and ultra-brief trunks is fine at resorts but not when visiting villages or shopping in town. At such times it is easy to take a *sulu* to use as a wraparound so no offence is caused.

Fiji enjoys a balmy tropical climate

Gleeful Fijian youngsters

Visa and Passports

A passport valid for at least three months beyond the intended period of stay and a ticket for onward travel is required. Tourist visas are granted on arrival, free of charge, for a stay of up to 30 days for citizens of Commonwealth countries and nationals of Austria, Belgium, Denmark, Finland, France, Greece, Iceland, Luxembourg, Nauru, Netherlands, Norway, Philippines, South Korea, Spain, Sweden, Switzerland, Taiwan, Thailand, Turkey, United States, Germany and Western Samoa. Nationals of other countries require pre-arranged visas. Tourist visas may be extended for up to six months on application to the Department of Immigration in Suva, Lautoka and Nadi or police stations in Ba, Tavua, Taveuni, Savusavu, Labasa and Levuka. It is necessary to have an onward ticket and sufficient funds. Those wishing to stay more than six months are advised to consult the Department of Immigration.

Vaccinations

Yellow fever and cholera vaccinations are only required if coming from an infected area. Hepatitis A and B jabs are advised.

Customs

After collecting their luggage, visitors will find two signs: NOTHING TO DECLARE and GOODS TO DECLARE. Those with nothing to declare will quickly find their way to the concourse outside the hall.

Electricity

The electrical current in Fiji is 240 volts AC 50HZ. Fiji has three-pin power outlets identical to those in Australia and New Zealand. If your appliances are 110v check for a 110/240v switch; if there is none you will need a voltage converter. Leading hotels and resorts generally offer universal outlets for 240v or 110v shavers, hairdryers etc.

Time Differences

Fiji is 12 hours ahead of GMT.
When it is 9am in Fiji, it is:

London	9pm	previous day
Frankfurt	10pm	previous day
New York	4pm	previous day
Los Angeles	1pm	previous day
Tokyo	6am	same day
Sydney	7am	same day
Auckland	9am	same day

GETTING ACQUAINTED

Geography

The 300 islands comprising the Republic of Fiji are located in the South-west Pacific between the latitudes 13° and 25° south and longitude 176° west and 177° east. It is an archipelago with the islands scattered across more than 517,998sq km (200,000sq miles) of the South Pacific Ocean. The islands of Tonga, Samoa and Vanuatu are nearby and New Zealand 2,253km (1,400 miles), and Australia 3,541km (2,200 miles) away are also not far. The two principal islands, Viti Levu with more than 10,360sq km (4,000sq miles) and Vanua Levu, 5,535sq km (2,137sq miles), comprise nearly 90 percent of the total land area. Most of Viti Levu is mountainous and Vanua Levu less so. The highest point is Mt Victoria, which is 1,323m (4,340ft) and is located at the northern tip of the Nadrau plateau in Viti Levu. The plateau has an average elevation above sea level of 900m (2,953ft). The highest point in Vanua Levu is Mt Dikeva which is 952m (3,123ft). The third largest island, Taveuni, is also geologically the youngest and owes its existence to volcanic action from Mt Uluiqalau, which at 1,241m (4,071ft), is the second highest in Fiji.

Cosmopolitan Fiji

Vanua Levu

Population and People

Fiji's population was estimated to be 738,000 at the end of 1989. Fijians total 363,000, Indians 340,100 and other races 35,000. The indigenous Fijian people are among some of the friendliest in the world and are so disarming that the first-time visitor often asks: 'Is this for real?' The friendliness is part of the culture which treats visitors as honoured guests. Most people will smile and say hello and invite strangers into their homes and villages. It is important not to take advantage of this friendship and hospitality.

Always reciprocate either by buying 500g of *yaqona* (the powdered root of a plant used for ritual drinking) or some food such as canned fish or corned beef. Do not go to villages dressed in brief shorts or swimsuits This is highly offensive to the locals. Despite the overall courtesy and friendliness, it pays to be cautious. There are some who will take advantage of tourists (see *Shopping*).

Religion

A multi-racial, multi-cultural nation, Fiji is represented by all the major religions of the world. This is quickly obvious to the visitor who will see Christian churches, Muslim mosques and Hindu temples in the towns and countryside. The majority of Fijians are of the Wesleyan persuasion, but all the other Christian denominations are represented. Sunday is observed as Sabbath with only minimal shops and services operating. Visitors are welcomed to Sunday worship.

Language

Due to its British colonial heritage, Fiji is an English-speaking country, although the two major races, Fijians and Indo-Fijians both speak in their vernacular. Ho-

Multi-ethnic Fiji

tel staff are fluent in the English language. The Wesleyan missionaries who first reduced the Fijian language to a written form were faced with a number of sounds peculiar to the language. For example, a Fijian will never say 'd' as in day. In the Fijian language the 'd' sound is always preceded by 'n' so that it will be an 'nd' as in Nandi. This also applies to 'b' which becomes 'mb'.

This is always confusing to visitors who will invariably keep mispronouncing many words such as Sigatoka, which is Singatoka, Beqa which is Bengga and the Mamanuca Islands are in fact the Mamanutha Islands. No wonder people are confused.

The following should be a help.

The vowels are pronounced as in the continental languages. The unusual consonant sounds are accounted thus:

B is 'mb' as in 'remember'
C is 'th' as in 'them'
D is 'nd' as in 'candy'
J is 'ch' as in 'church'
G is 'ng' as in 'singalong'
Q is 'g' as in 'great'

MONEY MATTERS

Currency

The Fijian dollar is the basic unit of currency. It is issued in 1, 2, 5, 10 and 20 dollar notes and 50, 20, 10, 5, 2 and 1 cent coins. Coins of 10, 20 and 50-cent value are most useful for telephones and parking meters.

Approximate exchange rate at time of publication, F$1 buys US66 cents. Exchange rates against all the major currencies are posted each day in all banks, listed in newspapers and displayed at most hotels. There is no limit on the amount of money brought in. Visitors are allowed to take out currency up to the amount imported.

Credits Cards and Banks

Major credit cards are welcomed by most hotels, restaurants, shops, rental car agencies, tours, cruises and travel agents. American Express, Diners Club, Visa, JCB International and Mastercard are represented in Suva. American Express can replace lost credit cards and travellers cheques.

Fiji is well represented by banking groups. These are, Australia and New Zealand group (ANZ Ltd), Bank of Baroda, National Bank of Fiji (NBF) and Westpac. All groups have head offices in Suva with branches and agencies throughout Fiji.

Business Hours

Normal business hours are from 9.30am to 3pm Monday to Thursday and till 4pm on Friday. There is a 24-hour bank service at the Nadi International Airport. Most shops and commercial outlets are open five days a week as well as Saturday mornings.

Tipping

Tipping is not encouraged in Fiji and it is left to the individual to determine whether or not to pay a gratuity. Though tipping is not a local custom, you will find local people tipping. This has much to do with social attitudes as it does in recognition of good service. Fijians ritually exchange gifts of food, clothing, *yaqona*, *tabua*, kerosene and even money during important social occasions, so tipping can be seen in the light of sharing.

Public bus

Bus

Fiji is a small country and the cost of getting about is not great, especially if you choose to travel by local transport. This comprises buses and 'carriers' – vans and 3-ton trucks, equipped with rudimentary seating that pick up and let off passengers as and where they find them. Bus companies offer express and normal services. With the express service, it is possible to go from Lautoka to Suva with stops only at Nadi, Sigatoka and Navua as well as at the hotels. Normal bus services will pick up and let off passengers where they find them. Carrier services are usually confined to their own area. The hotel travel desk will advise. Otherwise, contact Pacific Transport; Suva, Tel: 304366; Nadi, Tel: 700044; Lautoka, Tel: 660499; and Sigatoka, Tel: 500088. Sunbeam Transport; Suva, Tel: 382704; Lautoka, Tel: 662822; and Sigatoka, Tel: 500168. Tour companies offer more luxurious facilities – comfortable seating and air conditioning but at a higher price. Check with the tour desk.

Taxis are plentiful

Taxi

There is a profusion of taxis. There is none of the frustration of some other parts of the world when a taxi is never available when you want it. In Fiji, they come looking for you. Drivers will even approach you on the street. There is a 50 cent flag fall charge and thereafter 50 cents for each kilometre, which makes Fiji's taxis amongst the cheapest in the world. Each taxi is required by law to have a meter but many do not turn it on. Insist that the driver turns the meter on and if he refuses to comply, step out of the cab. Drivers will also happily make 'deals' for sightseeing and excursions for the day. A quick check with the nearest Fiji Visitors Bureau office or the hotel desk will confirm whether the 'deal' is in fact a good one.

Car

By world standards, rental cars are not cheap in Fiji, due in part to the extremely high rate of import duty levied by the Government on vehicles. Rental car companies are obliged to recover a good deal of the cost of the new vehicle within a two-year operating period before selling the car. It is possible to obtain an all-inclusive daily rate for under F$50 for a small car, but it is necessary to study carefully what is actually 'included'. As in all things, it pays in the long run to stick with brand names and Avis is one of the best known in Fiji for both its service and reliability. The company is represented in most of the leading hotels and at all the major centres, including Savusavu and Labasa in Vanua Levu. Contact numbers are: Nadi; Tel: 72233 (24-hour service) and Suva; Tel: 313833. Avis is also represented at all leading hotels.

Ferry

There are two major domestic shipping lines which service the islands of Ovalau, Gau, Koro, Vanua Levu, Viti Levu and Taveuni. These are Patterson Brothers and the Consort Shipping Line. Both companies operate large vessels and carry trucks and cars. For fare information call the Consort Shipping Line; Tel: 302877 and Patterson Brothers; Tel: 315644.

Domestic Air

Air Pacific, the designated national airline, concentrates on overseas flights and

Sunflower Airlines operates domestic flights

leaves the domestic routes to Fiji Air and Sunflower Airlines. All major islands are serviced by internal flights including a good number of outer islands like Kadavu, which is becoming an increasingly more popular destination for dedicated scuba divers. Fiji Air offers a special package of F$180 for a return flight to Levuka, Kadavu, Savusavu and Taveuni. It must be one of the best deals around the Pacific when considering that a one-way fare to Taveuni from Nadi is F$116.

ACCOMMODATION

There is no official rating for hotels and resorts in Fiji. Price is the only real indicator although it would be fair to say that the most expensive is not necessarily the best. On arrival at Nadi International Airport and through immigration, there is a listing of various hotels, resorts and budget accommodations with rack rates. The Fiji Visitors Bureau at the airport will help those who have made no prior bookings. Better deals are available through your travel agent or if there is time, in writing or faxing to see what the best offers are. There is no high or low season for room rates, though sometimes specials are offered during the months of February and March.

The following symbols indicate price ranges for a single standard room. All prices are subject to a government tax of 10 percent.

$	=	under F$50
$$	=	F$50–F$100
$$$	=	F$100–F$150
$$$$	=	F$150–F$200
$$$$$	=	F$200 and above

Nadi area

SHERATON FIJI RESORT
Denarau Island
Tel: 701777
300 ocean-view rooms are appointed with balconies overlooking the garden and the sea. There are four restaurants, two cocktail bars and a disco which attracts expatriates and locals on the weekends. Room rate includes a full buffet breakfast, complimentary non-motorised water sports and day-time tennis. The hotel is well run and the staff obliging and friendly. There is a large pool, pool bar and beach, and an adjoining 18-hole championship golf course, all-weather tennis courts and a host of daily activities. $$$$$

THE REGENT OF FIJI
Denarau Island
Tel: 780000
Tastefully understated rooms with Fijian motifs and a full range of facilities for dining and recreation. Good food and service, and friendly staff. $$$$$

RAFFLES GATEWAY HOTEL
Nadi Airport
Tel: 722444
Opposite the entrance to the Nadi International Airport and most convenient for transfers. Pleasant rooms and 24-hour courtesy bus to the airport. Pool, restaurant and coffee shop. $$

Mamanutha Islands

The Mamanutha Islands which feature superb white-sand beaches and watersports are just 10 minutes by air from Nadi International Airport. There is an airstrip on Malolo Lailai Island which has two resorts. It also serves as a pick-up point for the other nearby hotels. A sea plane and helicopter service are available for those who wish to fly direct to their island destination. Regular passenger ferries and high-speed water taxis service the resorts and Nadi each day.

BEACHCOMBER ISLAND RESORT
Tel: 662600
Tiny island full of fun. Caters to day trippers, backpackers and the young at heart who want to be part of the fun but would like to stay in their own *bure*. Prices are inclusive of all meals. $$

MUSKET COVE RESORT
Tel: 722488
Built by Dick Smith, father of Mamanutha Island resorts. Smith also built the nearby Castaway Island and Plantation Island Resorts. Musket Cove is on Malolo Lailai Island, the only one in the Mamanuthas with an airstrip. Accommodation in *bures* by the beach with cooking facilities. Restaurant, bar, general store and full range of activities. Attracts interesting people and yachtsmen who enjoy shore side facilities. $$$$

Sheraton Fiji

NAITASI RESORT
Malolo Island
Tel: 790178
Spacious accommodation in cottages with facilities which include cooking facilities. Full range of activities. $$$$

TAVARUA ISLAND RESORT
Tel: 723513
Surfers dream come true. Intimate environment-friendly resort with 12 *bures* and some of the best surfing waves in the world. $$$$

Coral Coast

This is a general term to describe the area from Momi Bay to Pacific Harbour on Viti Levu. In the days before the new highway was built, the road followed the coast from Momi most of the way. The area up to Korotogo, 6½km (4 miles) south of Sigatoka, is also on the 'dry' side of the island. There is a good range of places to stay which cater to all budgets. The nearby beach is good for swimming at high tide and for reef walking at low tide. Sovi Bay is only 7km (4¼ miles) away and offers excellent swimming all year through on the southern side.

87

SHANGRI-LA'S FIJIAN RESORT
Yanuca Island
Tel: 520155
436 rooms on its own island with an excellent beach, 9-hole golf course, full range of activities, five restaurants, seven bars and shopping arcade. For those who enjoy crowds. $$$$$

THE CROWS NEST
Queens Highway, Korotogo
Tel: 500230
Individual cottages with cooking facilities neatly arranged on the side of a hill overlooking the lagoon and ocean. Built by the late Paddy Doyle, one of Fiji's tourism personalities. Popular with locals and visitors alike. Restaurant, bar and pool. $$

THE NAVITI
Queens Highway, Korolevu
Tel: 500444
A pleasant retreat with nice beach, pool and a nearby small island. Full range of activities and helpful staff. $$$$

Pacific Harbour/Beqa Island
This area has long been the playground of Suva residents. It is only 49km (30½ miles) from the city, has the longest beach in Fiji and the nearby Beqa and Yanuca Islands offer some of the best fishing and diving in the world.

Typical bure-style accommodation

MARLIN BAY RESORT
Beqa Island
Tel: 304042
Relatively recent addition to Fiji's tourism industry and the first on Beqa island, just offshore from Pacific Harbour where the transfers are made. 12 beachside *bures*. Excellent for divers and fishermen. Good food and service. $$$

OCEAN PACIFIC CLUB
Queens Highway
Tel: 303252
Only resort catering to deep-sea fishermen. Small and intimate with only eight cottages. Full range of activities as well as fishing and diving. $$$

Suva
SUVA TRAVELODGE
Victoria Parade
Tel: 301600
Waterfront location within strolling distance of the heart of the city. Good service and accommodation, two restaurants and pool. $$$$

Outer Islands
This includes the nearby islands of Ovalau, Naigani, Kadavu, Toberua and Wakaya.

TOBERUA ISLAND RESORT
Lomaiviti
Tel: 479177
Small exclusive retreat with 12 beachside *bures* built in a style that honours the highest chiefs. All activities and excursions inclusive in the rates except scuba diving and deep sea fishing. $$$$$

Levuka
Former capital of Fiji on the island of Ovalau 10 minutes by air from Nausori Airport.

ROYAL HOTEL
Tel: 440024
Fiji's oldest hotel with some parts dating back to 1860. Rooms have ensuite facilities. Lovely atmosphere. Located just in front of a municipal market. $

View of Suva Travelodge

MAVIDA LODGE
Tel: 440051
Quiet, clean and inexpensive. Serves good home-cooked food. Probably the best value in Fiji. Conveniently located on Beach Street, which retains much of its old-world character. $

The North
This area includes Fiji's second largest island, Vanua Levu, and Taveuni which is the third largest. It includes a number of other nearby islands as well.

KON TIKI
Savusavu
Tel: 850262
Former banana, copra, pineapple and papaya plantation with a 9-hole golf course, swimming pool, tennis courts, bush walks and ocean-side activities. $$

MATAGI ISLAND
Taveuni
Tel: 880260
Only 10 *bures* on a 97-ha (240-acre) privately-owned island. Resort operated by the Douglas family with special interest in scuba diving, deep sea fishing and watersports. There is also a romantic tree-house for honeymooners. Beautiful island, lovely ambience. $$$

HEALTH & EMERGENCIES

Police
The Fiji Police Force is responsible for the maintenance of law and order and control of traffic. Police should be immediately contacted in all cases of crime and also for visa extension when away from Suva, Nadi, Lautoka and Levuka.

Telephone numbers are:

Suva	Tel: 311222
Lautoka	Tel: 660222
Labasa	Tel: 881222
Levuka	Tel: 440222
Nadi	Tel: 700222
Sigatoka	Tel: 500222
Nausori	Tel: 477222
Navua	Tel: 460222
Rakiraki	Tel: 694222
Savusavu	Tel: 850222
Taveuni	Tel: 880222.

Robbery
Fiji has a very low rate of crime against visitors but it makes sense to take intelligent precautions. It is sensible not to wander about alone in any of the urban areas late at night or in the early hours of the morning, especially when worse for wear because of drink. There have been cases of muggings but these are rare. It is also sensible for women not to seek out secluded beaches and go there alone.

More of a problem are 'sword sellers' and 'guides' who trade on the gullibility of visitors. (See *Shopping*.)

Accident and Illness

Fiji is free of major tropical diseases, including malaria. It has an effective, western-style medical system although local people still believe in the efficacy of age-old herbal remedies. The Government is encouraging an awareness of the importance of diet and hygiene to health, and for its part, supports the municipalities in the provision of safe drinking water. Fresh water reticulated in Suva, Lautoka and the other major towns are treated and is safe to drink from the tap. This also applies to hotels and resorts but not at villages. Some resorts use artesian water for bathing, but provide drinking water separately. If this is the case, visitors will be advised.

Hospitals are located in the major centres and there are health centres in rural areas. Hotels and resorts usually have a qualified nurse on the premises and a doctor on call. It is wise to take out a comprehensive health insurance.

Emergency numbers

Nadi – ambulance, Tel: 701128; hospital, Tel: 701128; police, Tel: 700222. Urgent pharmacy, Westside Drugs open Sunday 10am to noon and thereafter on call, Tel: 700310, 780188, 780044.

Suva – ambulance, Tel: 301439; hospital, Tel: 313444; police, Tel: 311222. Check with the hospital for the nearest rostered urgent pharmacy.

Lautoka – ambulance, Tel: 660399; hospital, Tel: 660399; police, Tel: 660222.

Check with the hospital for the nearest rostered urgent pharmacy.

MEDIA & COMMUNICATION

Postal Services

Post offices open from 8am and close at 4pm Monday to Friday at all the main centres. Letters address to c/o The Post Office at the designated area will be held for you and delivered on proof of identity. Telegram, fax and telephone services are also offered.

Telecommunications

Coin-operated telephone kiosks may be found outside main post offices. The services are operated by Fiji Post and Telecom, a government-owned corporation. Internal and external telephone calls are easily placed through your hotel which will also arrange to transmit your telex or facsimile messages. The country code for Fiji is 679. There are no area codes. Check with the operator for long distance and international charges, which may also be found in the telephone directory. Most of the major hotels have international direct dial facilities. The access code in Fiji is 05, followed by the country code: Australia (61); France (33); Germany (49); Italy (39); Japan (81); Netherlands (31); Spain (34); UK (44); US and Canada (1). If using a US credit phone card dial 012 and book your call with the operator. Dial 022 for international directory inquiries.

Media

The Fiji Times and *Post* are the two daily newspapers. The government, through the Fiji Broadcasting Commission, operates Radio Fiji in AM and FM frequencies in English, 1089AM and 104 FM; Hindi, 774AM and 98FM; and Fijian, 558AM. Broadcast times begin at 5pm and continue until 12 midnight. Radio Navtarang is an independent station operating on FM96 24 hours a day. Television New Zealand in association with the Fiji government operates a temporary television service in the Suva, Nadi and Lautoka areas. The Government is drafting tenders for a permanent service.

PHONES HIT BY TAX BLUNDER

Thursday, November 12, 1992

USEFUL ADDRESSES

The Fiji Hotel Association and the Society of Fiji Travel Agencies are the two leading industry bodies. Consumer complaints should be directed to the Consumer Council of Fiji or the appropriate industry association with a copy to the Fiji Visitors Bureau.

FIJI HOTEL ASSOCIATION
P.O. Box 13560
Suva, Fiji Islands
Tel: (679) 302980
Fax: (679) 300331

SOCIETY OF FIJI TRAVEL AGENCIES
P.O. Box 654
Suva, Fiji Islands
(Attn. The President)
Tel: (679) 302333
Fax: (679) 302048

CONSUMER COUNCIL OF FIJI
21 Stewart Street
Suva, Fiji Islands
Tel: (679) 300792

FIJI DIVE OPERATORS ASSOCIATION
P.O. Box 92
Suva, Fiji Islands
Tel: (679) 302433
Fax: (679) 300970

FIJI VISITORS BUREAU OFFICES
Head Office
Thomson Street
GPO Box 92
Suva, Fiji Islands
Tel: (679) 302433
Fax: (679) 300970
Telex: FJ2180 TOURIST

Nadi Airport Concourse
Box 9217
Nadi Airport
Tel: (679) 722433
Fax: (679) 790141

RECOMMENDED READING

Cyclopedia of Fiji Sydney 1907, reprinted by Fiji Museum, Suva, 1984, 1985.
Clunie, Fergus *Fijian Weapons and Warfare*, Fiji Museum, 1977.
Derrick, R.A. *A History of Fiji*, Suva 1946.
Lockerby, W. *The Journal of William Lockerby*, London, Hakluyt Society.
Siers, James *Fiji Celebration*, Suva 1986, 1990.
Siers, James *Blue Lagoons and Beaches*, Suva 1985, 1989, 1990.
Routledge, David *Matanitu: The struggle for power in early Fiji*, Suva 1985.
Williams, Thomas *Fiji and the Fijians vol. 1, The Islands and Their Inhabitants*, London 1958, reprinted Fiji Museum, Suva, 1982, 1983, 1984, 1985.

GLOSSARY

adi	A woman of chiefly rank
bete	A priest-cum-master of ceremonies
bilibili	Bamboo raft
Bula	Fijian greeting, more properly *ni sa bula vinaka*
Bure	Native style house with thatched roof. Many resorts adopt this style but furnish the interior with modern facilities.
bure kalou	Ancient temple
dalo	Taro or yam
kanikani	A condition induced by *yaqona*
lolo	Coconut milk
masi or *tapa*	Cloth made from a species of hibiscus tree specially cultivated for the purpose. The bark is stripped, soaked in water and then beaten out in varying degrees of thickness depending on the requirements of usage. Beautiful and ingenious decorations are then applied to the finished cloth. Sold in curio shops in various sizes. The National Museum has wonderful examples.
meke	Traditional communal dance/theatre
sevusevu	Gift for a guest
sulu	Rectangular piece of cloth
tabua	The tooth of the sperm whale presented on all important occasions, such as births, deaths, marriages, official and family requests etc. No Fijian ceremony of importance can be deemed to have taken place without the ritual presentation of *tabua*.
tanoa	Bowl for drinking *yaqona*
tavioka	Cassava (a tuber cultivated in the tropics)
turaga ni koro	Village headman, usually elected to the post. He is the chief executive of village affairs, overseeing all co-operative tasks.
vanua	Political confederation
vinaka	Thank you; good
vinaka vaka levu	Thank you very much
yaqona	The powdered root of the plant, piper mythisticum. This is mildly narcotic and is imbibed throughout Fiji by all races. As with the presentation of the *tabua*, *yaqona* is a must on all formal and even informal occasions. Visitors wishing to see a village which is not on a tour schedule, should always bring at least 500g of dried, unpounded roots to present to the *turaga ni koro*.

Index

A

accommodation 27, 28, 29, 39–40, 46, 56, 57, 60, 86–89
air, domestic 38, 39, 56, 85–86
archaeological discoveries 13, 34

B

Ba 36, 40
Ba River 35, 36
Baker, Reverend 52, 53, 54
Bau 15, 16, 61
Bavadra, Dr Timoci 24
Bay of Islands 29
Beachcomber Island 46
Beachcomber Island Resort 46–47
Beqa Island 28, 45
Bligh, Captain William 14, 19
Bligh Water 15, 37, 50
Blue Lagoon Cruise 48–49, 50–51
Bouma falls (Taveuni) 60
Bukuya 35, 38
Bulu Bay 27
bures 24, 27, 29, 36, 52, 60
Burr, Raymond 23, 24
buses 85
business hours 84

C

Cakaudrove 16
Cakobau, Ratu Seru 17, 19
cannibalism 14, 15, 29, 52

car hire 85
Cargill, David 19
Castaway Island 22
Catholic Church (Levuka) 39
climate 81
Colo war 19, 37
Cook, Captain James 14, 19
Coral Coast 21, 27
Coral Coast Railway 33
Costello, Dan 46
Cross, William 19
cruises 21–23, 48, 49–51
cuisine, Fijian 70–71
Cultural Centre (Pacific Harbour) 28
culture, Fijian 18

F

fauna 29
ferry 85
festivals 78–79
Fiji Museum 30
Fiji Visitors Bureau 78, 91
Fijians 18, 83
fishing 45, 47, 53, 56, 61, 64
flora 30
Forbes, Malcolm 59

G, H

Ganilau, Ratu Sir Penaia 59
Garden of the Sleeping Giant 23
Gatty, Harold 48
geography 82

golf 28, 33, 56, 59, 61
Government Handicraft Centre (Suva) 31
Government House (Suva) 30
Great Council of (Fijian) Chiefs 17, 18
handicrafts 31, 67
Heemskirk Reef 14, 19, 55
Honeymoon Island 22
Horse Shoe Bay 60

I, J, K

Indians 17, 19, 83
Japanese invasion 19, 30
jewellery 66–67
Kaba Peninsula 61
Keyasi (Sigatoka River Valley) 53
Kioa Island 55, 58
Kon Tiki Resort (Vanua Levu) 56
Korolevu Village 28, 54
Korotogo 27
Kubulau 57
Kulukulu sand dunes 34

L

Labasa (Vanua Levu) 55, 57
Lami 29
language 83–84
Laucala Island 55, 59
Lautoka 25
Lawai 37
Leluvia Island 39–40
Lesiaceva Point 56
Levuka (Ovalau Island) 16, 38–39, 61
Lockerby, William 16

M

Ma'afu 17, 19, 58
Malevu 27
Mamanutha Islands 32, 46–47
Market Place (Pacific Harbour) 28
Matagi Island 55, 60
media 91
Momi Bay 32

Motoriki Island 53
Municipal markets 31–32, 68–69

N

Na Koro 56
Nadarivatu 51
Nadi (Viti Levu) 20, 21, 75–76
Nadi International Airport 20, 46, 80
Naibose, Ilai 51, 53
Nakavu village 42
Nalebaleba 37
Namuamua Village 42, 44–45
Nasaucoko 37
Nasova 39
Natadola Beach 33
Natewa Bay 57
Nausori 35
Nausori Highlands 34–35
Navakacoa 59
Navala Village 36, 41
Naviti 28
Navo Island 33
Navua 28, 41
Nawi Island 56
nightlife 75–77
Nubutautau village 51–52, 54
Nukusere village 42

O, P, Q

Orchid Island 28
Ovalau Island 61
Pacific Harbour 28
population 17, 18, 83
public holidays 79
Qamea Island 55, 59, 60

R

Rabi Island 55, 57, 58
Rabuka, Major General Sitiveni 18
Ratu Sukuna Park 31, 32
religion 83
restaurants 25, 29, 32, 71–74

Rotuma 19
Rukua village 45

S

Sabeto Range 23
sandalwood trade 15, 19
Savage, Charlie 15, 16
Savusavu (Vanua Levu) 56, 57
scuba diving 47, 56, 61, 62–63
shopping 66–69
Sigatoka 27
Sigatoka River Valley 37
Simpson, Laurie 57
Slater, Olive 19
snorkelling 22, 23, 33, 45, 47, 49, 61
Somosomo 59
Sovi Bay 27
sugar cane 17, 19, 25, 32, 34, 37, 55
sugar mill 25, 36
Sukuna, Ratu Sir Lala 19
Suva 19, 26, 29, 76–77

T

Tasman, Abel 14, 19
Tavagia, Ratu Sir Josaia 24
Taveuni Island 19, 55, 57, 58, 83
taxis 85
telecommunications 90
Thurston Gardens 30
time zones 82

Toberua Island 60
Toberua Island Resort 60–61
Tongan Fort (Naroro) 27, 37
Totoga Falls (Levuka) 39
Tui Vuda 24, 25
Tuva Indian School 32
Tuvamila 57

U, V

University of the South Pacific 30
Vanua Levu 19, 20, 55, 83
Vatoa Island 19
Vatukarasa 27
Vaturu dam 35
Viseisei Village 24–25
Viti Levu 20, 51, 55, 83
Vuda Point 24

W, Y

Wairiki 58
Waiyevo (Taveuni) 58
Walu Bay 29
Waya 50
Whippy, David 16
whitewater rafting 36, 40
windsurfing 33, 34, 47, 61
Withers, Trever 48, 49
Yanuca Island 28
yaqona 36, 42, 45, 54, 68–69, 83
Yasawa Islands 25, 37, 48–50

ART & PHOTO CREDITS

Photography	
Cover, Backcover	**James Siers**
49T	**Topham Picture Source**
12, 13, 14/15, 16, 17	**Caines-Jannif Collection**
Handwriting	**V Barl**
Cover Design	**Klaus Geisler**
Cartography	**Berndtson & Berndtson**
Senior Desktop Operator	**Suriyani Ahmad**

INSIGHT GUIDES

COLORSET NUMBERS

160 Alaska	204 East African Wildlife	100 New England
155 Alsace	149 Eastern Europe,	184E New Orleans
150 Amazon Wildlife	118 Ecuador	184F New York City
116 America, South	148A Edinburgh	133 New York State
173 American Southwest	268 Egypt	293 New Zealand
158A Amsterdam	123 Finland	265 Nile, The
260 Argentina	209B Florence	120 Norway
287 Asia, East	243 Florida	124B Oxford
207 Asia, South	154 France	147 Pacific Northwest
262 Asia, South East	135C Frankfurt	205 Pakistan
194 Asian Wildlife,	208 Gambia & Senegal	154A Paris
Southeast	135 Germany	249 Peru
167A Athens	148B Glasgow	184B Philadelphia
272 Australia	279 Gran Canaria	222 Philippines
263 Austria	169 Great Barrier Reef	115 Poland
188 Bahamas	124 Great Britain	202 Portugal
206 Bali Baru	167 Greece	114A Prague
107 Baltic States	166 Greek Islands	153 Provence
246A Bangkok	135G Hamburg	156 Puerto Rico
292 Barbados	240 Hawaii	250 Rajasthan
219B Barcelona	193 Himalaya, Western	177 Rhine
187 Bay of Naples	196 Hong Kong	127A Rio de Janeiro
234A Beijing	144 Hungary	172 Rockies
109 Belgium	256 Iceland	209A Rome
135A Berlin	247 India	101 Russia
217 Bermuda	212 India, South	275B San Francisco
100A Boston	128 Indian Wildlife	130 Sardinia
127 Brazil	143 Indonesia	148 Scotland
178 Brittany	142 Ireland	184D Seattle
109A Brussels	252 Israel	261 Sicily
144A Budapest	236A Istanbul	159 Singapore
260A Buenos Aires	209 Italy	257 South Africa
213 Burgundy	213 Jamaica	264 South Tyrol
268A Cairo	278 Japan	219 Spain
247B Calcutta	266 Java	220 Spain, Southern
275 California	252A Jerusalem-Tel Aviv	105 Sri Lanka
180 California, Northern	203A Kathmandu	101B St Petersburg
161 California, Southern	270 Kenya	170 Sweden
237 Canada	300 Korea	232 Switzerland
162 Caribbean	202A Lisbon	272 Sydney
The Lesser Antilles	258 Loire Valley	175 Taiwan
122 Catalonia	124A London	112 Tenerife
(Costa Brava)	275A Los Angeles	186 Texas
141 Channel Islands	201 Madeira	246 Thailand
184C Chicago	219A Madrid	278A Tokyo
151 Chile	145 Malaysia	139 Trinidad & Tobago
234 China	157 Mallorca & Ibiza	113 Tunisia
135E Cologne	117 Malta	236 Turkey
119 Continental Europe	272B Melbourne	171 Turkish Coast
189 Corsica	285 Mexico	210 Tuscany
281 Costa Rica	285A Mexico City	174 Umbria
291 Cote d'Azur	243A Miami	237A Vancouver
165 Crete	237B Montreal	198 Venezuela
184 Crossing America	235 Morocco	209C Venice
226 Cyprus	101A Moscow	263A Vienna
114 Czechoslovakia	135D Munich	255 Vietnam
247A Delhi, Jaipur, Agra	211 Myanmar (Burma)	267 Wales
238 Denmark	259 Namibia	184C Washington DC
135B Dresden	269 Native America	183 Waterways
142B Dublin	203 Nepal	of Europe
135F Düsseldorf	158 Netherlands	215 Yemen

You'll find the colorset number on the spine of each Insight Guide.